**IF YOU'RE AT THE THEATRE AND
HAVE JUST PICKED THIS BOOK UP**

This diagram is a quick guide to how the
relate to each other. If yo
front of DURING (p.25) for

RELATIONSHIP CIRCLE

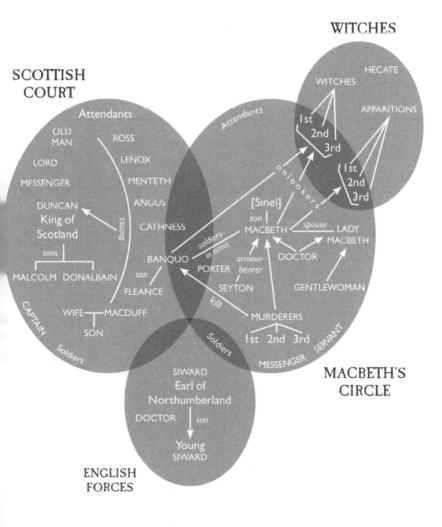

Springboard Shakespeare Series

Ben Crystal

Advisory Editor, Professor Michael Dobson, Shakespeare Institute, University of Birmingham

Macbeth
King Lear
Hamlet
A Midsummer Night's Dream

Further titles in preparation

ARDEN SHAKESPEARE
SPRINGBOARD SHAKESPEARE

MACBETH

BEFORE | DURING | AFTER

BEN CRYSTAL

B L O O M S B U R Y
LONDON • NEW DELHI • NEW YORK • SYDNEY

Bloomsbury Arden Shakespeare

An imprint of Bloomsbury Publishing Plc

50 Bedford Square
London
WC1B 3DP
UK

1385 Broadway
New York
NY 10018
USA

www.bloomsbury.com

First published 2013

© Ben Crystal, 2013
Map on p.22 Copyright © Kate Bellamy, 2013

Ben Crystal has asserted his right under the Copyright, Designs and
Patents Act, 1988, to be identified as Author of this work.

British Library Cataloguing-in-Publication Data
A catalogue record for this book is available from the British Library.

ISBN: PB: 978-1-4081-6462-4

Library of Congress Cataloging-in-Publication Data
A catalog record for this book is available from the Library of Congress

Typeset by Fakenham Prepress Solutions, Fakenham, Norfolk NR21 8NN

CONTENTS

How best to use this book   vi

Series preface   vii

Before   1

During   25

After   77

Glossary   99

HOW BEST TO USE THIS BOOK

If you've just picked it up and you're heading into the theatre:
Take a quick look at the Relationship Circle on the inside front cover. It will give you a quick reference guide to how the characters in the play you're about to see or read relate to each other; the list of characters is on the inside back cover

- at the Interval, take a look at the Five Interval Whispers (p.26)
- and just in case, the last pages of the book are a dictionary of all the difficult words in the play
- then on your way home, read through the AFTER section, which is written as a more advanced, in-depth discussion of some of the characters and issues in the play. I make reference to other characters in other Shakespeare plays but no prior knowledge of these others is necessary

If you're about to read the play, then
- read the BEFORE section. It gives all the essential information you need about the way Shakespeare writes, and explains some of the trickier aspects of the play. It also explains the conventions of the DURING section
- the DURING section looks at theatrically interesting parts of each scene to watch out for. Important character choices or difficult words and phrases are provided, and the major speeches in the play are broken down and annotated as an actor might do in a rehearsal script
- then dive into the AFTER section

If you're about to watch a film of the play, then the DURING section can be used like a DVD commentary

The book, as the title of the series suggests, is not meant to be comprehensive. The opinions are my own, and are just that – opinions. I hope they'll provoke some healthy disagreement

SERIES PREFACE

Shakespeare was written to be learnt. To be spoken out loud. So what are the things it would be useful to know before reading or watching a Shakespeare play? What few pieces of information can help turn it from being a famous work of literature into an exciting, thrilling piece of drama? What does *this* Shakespeare play mean here, tonight, now?

And when it's over, what next? These plays have been performed for over four hundred years, and they're still being performed because they're open to such wide interpretation when it comes to staging them. Directors and actors need to find their own answers to the questions which Shakespeare's scripts leave wide open:

– is Hamlet actually mad or only pretending to be?
– is the Fool in *King Lear* an old man or a young boy?
– how old are the Witches in *Macbeth*? What kind of costume should they wear?
– at what point does Orlando realise the truth about Rosalind in *As You Like It*?
– does Isabella agree to marry the Duke in *Measure for Measure*?

The last is one of my favourites: Isabella, wanting to join a nunnery, is nearly forced to have sex with the manipulative Angelo, but is saved by the rightful Duke. Everything is resolved, and the Duke ends the play announcing he will propose to Isabella – but Shakespeare doesn't give her a vocal response. So how should she react? Should she agree to marry the Duke, refuse, or give no answer and leave the play with the open question?

There are no definitively right or wrong answers to these types of questions, but one of the addictive things about a Shakespeare play is knowing that those questions are there at all, and coming up with your own answers. Or going to see a production and seeing how a company of players tries to answer them for you. Then going to see another production of the same play, to see how differently *that* company answers those questions.

Measure could be performed many ways. If Isabella agrees, perhaps the actors choose to show that a love has been blossoming between her and the Duke throughout the play, and she rejects the life of a nun. If she refuses, perhaps it's because the life of a nun is the only one for her. Or does the play end with the dilemma: the life of a nun, or life as a Duchess with the man who saved her…?

And this is just *one* moment at the very end of what many consider to be a fairly tricky play. It's this tantalisingly elusive quality that keeps people producing Shakespeare's plays, and everyone who plays Hamlet, or Macbeth, or Isabella will answer these questions differently.

In this series, then, you will be guided through Shakespeare's works towards particular passages and key moments to watch out for, and – much as in a rehearsal room – nudged to consider why it might be there.

This series is not a one-stop shop, a Shakespearean supermarket where you can read up on everything you need to know about a particular play. You will not find a theme-by-theme dissection here, nor a comprehensive, definitive analysis.

Rather, using different exploratory techniques throughout, we will look at the bare bones of the play, some of the questions Shakespeare has left us, and the theatrical world in which Shakespeare was writing, offering answers to hang on the skeleton. We'll see how these questions have been answered in the past, and where in the world of Shakespeare we can go next.

This is a springboard into Shakespeare.

Ben Crystal

With thanks to:

Michael Dobson, Eric Rasmussen, James Shapiro, James Mardock, and Rob Gander, for their notes

Dan Winder and www.IrisTheatre.com; Roberta Brown; and the actors Emma Pallant, Laura Wickham, David Baynes, Jamie Harding, Warren Rusher, Diana Kashlan, Anwar Kashlan, Matthew Mellalieu, Benjamin O'Mahoney, Damien Molony, Hilton McRae, William Sutton, and all at www. PassionInPractice.com, for the spectacular insights I pilfered

Anthony Del Col at *Kill Shakespeare!* and Kerstin Twachtmann, for their design suggestions

Kate Bellamy for the beautiful maps

My editor Margaret Bartley; Terry Woodley, Suzi Williamson, Hilary Schan, Claire Cooper, Emily Hockley and all at Arden and Bloomsbury; Kim and all at Fakenham Prepress

Cathryn Summerhayes and Becky Thomas at William Morris Endeavor

Mum and Dad, Jim, Kate, for their notes and endless support

BEFORE

Tony Montana: Me, I want what's coming to me.
Manny: Oh, well what's coming to you?
Tony Montana: The world, chico, and everything in it.

Scarface (1983)

If you haven't seen it, *Macbeth* is image-famous for witches, a floating dagger, and the midnight murder of a Scottish king.

Beyond these, it's a blood-soaked play with unspeakable brutality – throat-slitting, decapitation, the killing of an innocent mother and child which is nothing less than horrific, the murder of three people while they sleep, the splitting of someone from stomach to jawbone with a sword, a possible suicide, and a few other deaths which make the on- and off-stage body count at least a dozen.

There are bloody ghosts, witches, and figures from the Greek Underworld – all ideas that would have brought terror to the minds of Shakespeare's audience. Characters hallucinate, are drugged, and are so terrified of their leader that they flee from their home and country. Some are so opposed to the dictator-like, tyrannical killing of innocents that they raise an army and go to war.

For Shakespeare's audience, the presence of witches and the main plotline of killing a king were topical as well as terrifying. Shakespeare was writing in a period of persecution known as the European Witch Craze, where many women (and men) were put under trial and executed under suspicion of witch-craft. In 1603, the Scottish King James VI acceded the English throne as King James I. A few years before, he had written a book about witches. And in 1605 (a few months before *Macbeth* was first performed) he survived an assassination attempt by Guy Fawkes and his co-conspirators.

MONARCH

The King or Queen was officially considered to be God's voice on Earth, and the removal of the rightful monarch meant anarchy, that the skies would darken and fall. This in a time when superstition was still so powerful that the existence of Pixies, Faeries and Ghosts were a commonly held belief by the average audience member, while an equally very religious world thought earthquakes to be the punishing Hand of God.

It's one of the most regularly produced plays of the 39 Shakespeare plays known to exist. First performed in 1606, *Macbeth* is a play about political and social instability, how far someone will go for power, and what that can cost. Not a million miles away from Al Pacino's movie, *Scarface* (see AFTER, p.95).

Macbeth is an incredible character to play. He experiences a rocket-rise to absolute power via murder, then plummets into absolute disaster, a roller-coaster ride turned runaway train. The loyal soldier who embraces his inner darkness, reaching the point of near-insanity, megalomania, paranoia and greed, who swings from uncertain weakness to a Superman-like conviction of invincibility.

The play was published 17 years after its first performance, in a collection compiled by two actors who had worked with Shakespeare throughout his time in London.

Originally called *Mr William Shakespeares Comedies, Histories & Tragedies* but often referred to as the *First Folio*, the collection was published in 1623, seven years after his death. It gave people the chance to own 18 of Shakespeare's plays that had never been printed before, including *Macbeth*.

The plays were written to be performed by a skilled team of craftsmen (women weren't allowed to act until half a century later) that the writer worked with for over 15 years – they've been referred to as 'Shakespeare's understanders like never before or since'.

They were meant to be learnt, and performed live – the best form of introduction is to see one acted. The characters speak directly to us, sharing the present moment, but at the same time half-belonging in a story that's been told many times over the centuries. So while *reading* a Shakespeare play can be a struggle, understanding the shorthand Shakespeare used to help his actors can help a modern audience more easily break open the plays.

Macbeth is a tricky play to do well. The parts are hard to play, there's an (often unfunny) comic monologue, the Witches are difficult to make scary, and late in the play there's a pause in the action that can make modern audiences switch off.

Done well, it can be absolutely terrifying. In the 1970s, Trevor Nunn directed the Ian McKellen/Judi Dench production at the Royal Shakespeare

Company (see AFTER, p.95). A priest was so spooked by the performance that he returned whenever he could and sat at the front, a crucifix in his hand, protecting the cast from the evil he believed they were raising.

It is the only play Shakespeare wrote that includes ghosts, apparitions *and* witches, and the only play of his considered to be actually cursed.

MACBETH IS CURSED

The most widely known 'fact' about the play is that there is a curse on it. Many theatre practitioners think that if the name of the play or title character is spoken outside of a performance or a rehearsal, it's bad luck. Instead, it's more often referred to as *The Scottish Play*.

It has this reputation not without good reason. Over the last few hundred years, a number of productions have apparently fallen foul of The Curse. Actors have been maimed, have died, and have killed each other during productions of *Macbeth*.

In John Gielgud's 1942 production, three actors died – Duncan, and two of the witches – and the set designer committed suicide. In 2001 in a production in Cambridge, Macduff injured his back, Lady Macbeth hit her head, Ross broke his toe, and two cedar trees crashed to the ground, destroying the set.

Of course, the play isn't actually cursed: *there's no such thing*, as Macbeth says at one point. But the story of the curse brings a peculiar modern flavour to what was one of the most political pieces of drama that came out of the 1600s, thanks to Shakespeare making use of the current events in his life to startling effect.

> *If you do* Macbeth *and you don't believe in witches, then, you know, why do the play?*
>
> **Mark Rylance, Actor and ex-Artistic Director of the reconstructed**
> **Shakespeare's Globe**

THE THEATRE

If you're going to see a staged production of *Macbeth*, it's likely that the environment that you see it in will be very different from the way Shakespeare's audience first saw it. Once, it would have been performed around 2pm in an outdoor theatre with people standing around the stage; or outdoors in the yard of a tavern; or in a hall at Court, at one of the monarch's palaces. The legal fiction was that any performance at a public theatre was technically a rehearsal and preparation, before showing the play to the royal patron. Still, many of Shakespeare's plays were first performed at the Globe theatre, an open-roofed, octagonal space on the south bank of the River Thames in London.

A reconstruction of the original theatre opened in 1997 (a hundred metres away from the original site) which tries to recreate the experience Shakespeare's audience would have had when the plays were performed in the afternoon. The lack of a roof over the yard allows the matinees to be lit by daylight; the stage is artificially lit at night, but only to simulate bright daylight.

Modern Shakespeare productions are more often staged in outdoor amphi-theatres, black-box studio theatres, proscenium-arch theatres (where the line between the audience and the stage is very clear), old warehouses, or just about anywhere else you could imagine, and the type of theatre will have a direct effect on the production.

Depending on how well-funded or literal-minded the theatre is, there might be lighting and sound effects to replicate a stormy night; the actors playing the Witches may have their voices distorted or amplified with microphones; or there may only be simple make-up and musical instruments used.

Some modern productions will encourage audience interaction, with pantomime-like asides (when the actors talk directly to the spectators), though this tends to happen more when the audience is surrounding the stage (in the round) or on either side (in the traverse). At the reconstructed Globe the actors often enter or exit through the yard, and sometimes act out scenes in it, amongst the audience. Similarly, in the RSC's Elizabethan-style indoor theatres in Stratford-upon-Avon, there are walkways built in through the audience area for the actors to use, equally giving the impression of watching the action from within the world of the play.

THE PLAY

Shakespeare's play is loosely based on the real historical events of 11th-century Scotland, but a modern production may well have relocated the action to a different time or place. As we'll see in the AFTER section of the book, the play is built around the characters, rather than the setting.

King Duncan and his generals are fighting the Scottish Thanes Cawdor and Macdonwald, who have aligned themselves with Sweno, the King of Norway.

One of Duncan's generals, Macbeth, meets three witches as he returns from battle. The Witches tell him he will become king. He relates their prediction to his wife, and together they plot to murder King Duncan. They kill Duncan as he sleeps in their castle, redirect suspicion away from them, and are crowned King and Queen. Macbeth becomes a tyrant, Lady Macbeth goes mad, and they end both dying quite unpleasant deaths.

Women and men in Shakespeare's time could be put on trial and executed for witchcraft or simply associating with suspected witches. Somewhere in the region of 60,000–120,000 women were executed for witchcraftery: Witches were a very real nightmare for Shakespeare's audience. They are to the modern world too. From 2006–12, according to the Legal and Human Rights Centre, thousands of women were lynched by villagers in Tanzania, terrified that they were witches.

As for the killing of a king, this was something Shakespeare had written about earlier on in his career with his *Henry VI* plays, with *Richard II* and

Richard III, and with *Hamlet*. It's an idea he kept coming back to: the monarch was thought to be a single step down from God. Commit an act against the monarch, and you're committing an act against God. Plot to murder the monarch, and you're essentially plotting to murder God. And if you murder the monarch to become the monarch, then you essentially become God on Earth... These were terrible, treasonous thoughts and – with the Guy Fawkes conspiracy – something Shakespeare's audience had nearly recently witnessed.

Guy Fawkes and his co-conspirators tried to destroy the Houses of Parliament with King James inside. They failed, were executed for treason – and a few months later Shakespeare's new play, featuring witchcraft and a successful assassination of a king, was performed. For his audience, *Macbeth* would have been one of the most topical, thrilling, socially relevant pieces of theatre they'd ever seen (*The Tragedy of Gowrie*, a 1604 play about a planned assassination of James I, had already been performed but then suppressed).

Macbeth is a play about what drives people to extraordinary lengths: ambition, fear, and fate, while looking at the wider struggle of holding a kingdom together under one authoritative power.

For Shakespeare's audience, there would be two possible outcomes of Duncan's murder. Either the Macbeths would get away with it and unrightfully be King and Queen, God's incarnation on Earth. Or if their treason was exposed and their opponents mustered sufficient force, they would be killed as murderous traitors. Macbeth would be hung, drawn and quartered, as Lady Macbeth would be hanged or burnt alive at the stake.

Either way, witches were thought to be in league with the Devil, so by listening to them Macbeth and Lady Macbeth are damning themselves forever, risking everything for absolute power.

SHAKESPEARE'S WORDS

If you're reading the play, it's worth bearing in mind this fact: the plays really were not intended to be read. It's said that 80 per cent of Shakespeare's original audience couldn't read, and if you're not used to reading them, they can be daunting when you open the book for the first time.

There's a common idea that the plays are full of difficult words, and he was writing in a different language. But only 5 per cent of all the words in Shakespeare's works are difficult for a modern audience to understand, and he was writing in an early version of modern English, so not *that* much has changed.

Still, the plays are four centuries old now, so some words have changed their meaning, and we need to know what they are. The quick-reference glossary at the back of the book will help with these.

Shakespeare was writing for an audience with a different educational and cultural background, and so some references do need to be explained. When Ross tells Duncan of the battle, he describes Macbeth as *Bellona's bridegroom*.

Knowing that Bellona was the Roman goddess of war makes the image of Macbeth's fighting ability a little clearer.

Shakespeare was the inventor – or at least the first recorded user – of over a thousand words in the English language that we still use today. He had a great gift for linguistic creation, taking a word that already existed like *assassin*, and reinventing it, making *assassination*. When Macbeth speaks this word in Act 1 Scene 7, his audience would have been excited to hear it for the first time in their lives; it would have kept them on their toes, listening keenly.

In the same way, when we hear unfamiliar words in a Shakespeare play they can be both exciting and challenging. There are signs that Shakespeare was well aware that some of his new words were going to be difficult for an audience to grasp – the unusual word *incarnadine* (= blood-red) is used to describe the *multitudinous seas* but is immediately explained: *this my hand will rather / The multitudinous seas incarnadine, / Making the green one red.*

The names of people and places can take us by surprise too – the noblemen are sometimes referred to using the places where their clans are located, such as *Glamis* for Macbeth, *Cawdor* for the rebellious Thane of Cawdor, and *Fife* for Macduff.

There are several geographical locations mentioned too, and the Map (p.22) is a guide to where the action takes place.

SHAKESPEARE'S THEATRE

The original Globe was a roundish building – in his *Henry V*, Shakespeare describes his theatre as 'a wooden O' – and the audience sat or stood around three sides of the stage. The cheapest entrance fee would let you stand near the stage. These audience members (referred to by Hamlet as 'the groundlings') would be packed in there, along with prostitutes, beer-sellers and pick-pockets. The most expensive seats were in the upper gallery, farthest from the stage, nearer to the fresh air and away from the hustle and bustle.

Despite the dramatic conclusion of the film *Shakespeare in Love* when Queen Elizabeth is seen to watch a play at a public theatre, the monarch would never have deigned to visit such a place. As they were referred to at the time, the theatres were the home of 'rogues and vagabonds' and often doubled as venues for the 'sport' of bear-baiting (tying a bear up and letting dogs attack it until it died; during the final battle, Macbeth says he feels like he has been bound to a stake, ready to be baited like a bear).

The plays would be performed at about two o'clock in the afternoon, so for any scenes set at night – and many of the scenes in *Macbeth* are – the actors would have to act as though it's dark, probably carrying flaming torches.

Shakespeare didn't ever prescribe an interval: it was the normal course of Elizabethan open-air theatres like the Globe to run the play through without one – refreshments (beer and nuts) were sold throughout. Later in his career Shakespeare's company would also play at the indoor Blackfriars Theatre – here there would be a brief interval after every act, to lower the chandeliers and refresh the candles, but no other fixed place for a longer break was set in the script.

Macbeth is one of his shortest plays, and an interval is a tricky thing to place even in a longer play. Recently, some productions have placed a break at the beginning of Act 3, before Macbeth and Lady Macbeth's entrance as King and Queen, though many more run the play without an interval at all (but with cuts made to the text). Indeed, the ferocious action can make the play feel like it wants to sprint on to the end without pause.

COMEDY, TRAGEDY, HISTORY...

As well as being one of the shortest, *Macbeth* is also one of the darkest plays, but there's great humour to be found in it. It's often played as a tragedy with little-to-no comedy, and even the main 'comic' part, the Porter, can be played as a dark, tragic, demon-figure. But as with all of Shakespeare's plays, there's an inherent balance of comedy and tragedy written in.

He knew, as the classic image of theatre (the *persona* mask) implies, that comedy and tragedy work best next to each other. A balanced play is key: if you make the audience laugh, it'll be easier to make them cry, and vice-versa. So don't be surprised if there are unexpected laughs, or if it has a black-comedy focus, instead of feeling like a 'pure' tragedy.

HELL – THE PORTER, 'SEYTON', AND MACBETH'S FINAL DESTINATION

The Porter is a famous character in the play who has a speech calling on ideologies and gags well known to Shakespeare's audience. He jokes that he's the porter to the gate to Hell, and perhaps he is. By killing the King in their castle, the Macbeths have essentially opened the doors to Hell.

Because the jokes are topical, and tied to recent current events in Shakespeare's life (see DURING, pp.48–9), he's a tricky part to play and make sense of. To counter this, modern productions add all kinds of stage business – from improvising new (equally topical) jokes, to keeping the original lines but making the audience laugh between the lines by clowning around.

It's a speech that has attracted debate – some people think it shouldn't be in the play at all, being too 'low' an interlude in a 'high' play. However, after the intense and brutal scene between Macbeth and Lady, the mass discovery of Duncan's murder and the ensuing grief that follows, Shakespeare (the master dramatist) knew his audience would appreciate a little light relief. So in order to maximise the tragedy of these scenes, Shakespeare inserts a moment of comedy.

There again, it's not just a comic interlude. On a practical level, the scene gives an opportunity for the blood-soaked actors playing the Macbeths to change and wash. On a more symbolic level, if the Porter represents Macbeth's castle as Hell then he reinforces the unsettling, supernatural element in the play. Indeed, some productions extend the part of the Porter to include the lines later used by the servant character Seyton. To an audience's ear, it might sound as if Macbeth has grown so evil that even a minion of Hell is serving him.

In terms of the speech being topical, the Porter speaks of an *equivocator* (someone who intentionally misuses one word for another to deceive the listener). Equivocation was at the front of the minds of Shakespeare and his audience. Father Garnet, a Jesuit priest, was hanged in May 1606 for his part in the Gunpowder plot of 5 November 1605. At his trial, he was famously discovered to have sworn evidence to be true that he knew in his mind was false – so trying to equivocate his way out of guilt.

The idea of equivocation underpins the play: the prophecies the Witches give to Macbeth seem to be straightforward, but turn out to have a double meaning – lies masquerading as truths – and doom him.

SIDE-NOTE

Over the course of his career, Shakespeare worked with two clowns in his troupe of actors. The first, Will Kemp, was a brilliant physical comic; the second, Robert Armin, was much more the melancholic clown and singer.

When Kemp left in 1599 Shakespeare's comedic characters go through a shift, the clown personality shifting in harmony with the shift in company members. It's said the replacement clown Armin would have improvised around the lines written for the Porter, and some modern productions allow their actor to do the same.

SHAKESPEARE'S LINES

I'm going to introduce Shakespeare's writing style through acting eyes. It's more often examined with a literary bent, but as his writing was originally created to be committed to memory for actors to perform, they can be more easily accessible using techniques familiar to the theatrical world.

Shakespeare's writing comes in several forms, and an understanding of the two main varieties is crucial: he writes in *prose*, which is a theatrical reflection of everyday speech, and he writes in poetry, organising a character's speech into rhythmical lines of *verse*.

You don't *have* to understand the way verse works – and how Shakespeare used it to direct his actors – in order to enjoy the plays, but if you do, it will change the way you read Shakespeare forever.

Most of the characters in *Macbeth* speak in verse – only 6.5 per cent of the lines in the play are prose. We hear the Porter, the Scottish Doctor, and Lady Macbeth's Waiting-gentlewoman speak in prose, as well as Lady Macduff and her Son, and the Witches, too, from time to time. Prose is the speech form that Shakespeare's lower-class characters usually use. Upper-class characters can speak in prose, but when they do, they're often consciously choosing to use the more colloquial level of speech, and sometimes switching from one to the other within the same scene depending on who they're speaking to, or what they're speaking about.

There were many kinds of poetic style available to Shakespeare, and by the time he wrote Macbeth he was very much in command of them all (more on this later). The Scottish noblemen and the witches both speak in verse, but they do so in very different ways.

The noblemen use the form of verse that was most popular in Shakespeare's lifetime: *iambic pentameter*. This was understood to be a line of rhythmical poetry (*metre*) with 10 syllables, made up of five (*penta*) stronger *DUM* beats and five weaker *de* ones, with the stronger beat every second syllable: de-**DUM** (known as an *iambic* rhythm).

Rather than write de-**DUM**, another way of annotating these beats is with an *x* for the weaker beat, and a \ for the stronger. So a line of iambic pentameter can look like this:

de-**DUM** de-**DUM** de-**DUM** de-**DUM** de-**DUM**

Or this.

x   \   x   \   x   \   x   \   x   \

They say the saxophone is the instrument closest in sound to the human voice; iambic pentameter is the writing closest in rhythm to spoken English, and its weak-strong beat pushes the speaker towards the more important syllables in a line. In its most regular form, we hear it when we first see Macbeth, who says to Banquo:

So **foul**   and **fair**   a   **day**   I   **have** not   **seen**
de-**DUM** de-**DUM** de-**DUM** de-**DUM** de-**DUM**

Note how close this is to the natural rhythm of English:

I   **went**   to **town**   to **buy**   a   **coat**   today
de-**DUM** de-**DUM** de-**DUM** de-**DUM** de-**DUM**
x   \   x   \   x   \   x   \   x   \

This length of line of can be easily said with one intake of breath, and the regular heartbeat-like rhythm makes it easy to commit to memory. As we'll see, it's also a poetic style that is easy to manipulate. And Shakespeare used it to delve into the heart and the mind, and explore what it is to be human.

CHARACTERFUL SPEECH

I mentioned above that Shakespeare wrote his characters' speech in several different forms. These forms are used to give notes on the character or the subject they're talking about. Low-status characters speak in prose, a form of writing reflecting normal speech. More important characters, or more important subject matter, are given a form of speech with more style – it's stylistically heightened speech, essentially, more poetic. Look at it this way:

Regular speech – **prose** – often used amongst low-status characters

> **SON**
> If he were dead, you'd weep for him; if you would
> not, it were a good sign that I should quickly have a new
> father.

Heightened speech – **iambic pentameter**, aka **verse**, aka **blank** (because it doesn't rhyme) **verse** – often used amongst high-status characters, and easy to spot by the capital letters at the beginning of each line

> **KING**
> This castle hath a pleasant seat; the air
> Nimbly and sweetly recommends itself
> Unto our gentle senses.

Very heightened speech – **rhyming verse** – often used amongst high-status characters in important moments

> **MACBETH**
> (*aside*)
>   Come what come *may*,
> Time and the hour runs through the roughest *day*.

We don't encounter it in *Macbeth*, but in other plays he gave characters a speech style that is even more heightened than rhyming verse – using the structure of an English poem called a **sonnet**. Higher than the sonnet is **song**, used to summon Hecate away in 3:5 (see AFTER, p.84).

Rhyming couplets can be indicators of particular *types* of important moments. Listen out for these couplets – they're not just poetry and nice on the ear – sometimes they're used to indicate a character is exiting, or wanting to exit:

> **MALCOLM**
>   Therefore to horse,
> And let us not be dainty of leave-taking,
> But shift away. There's warrant in that *theft*
> Which steals itself when there's no mercy *left*.
>
> *Exit.*

Also, English pronunciation has changed over the last 400 years, so bear the following example from the end of the play in mind if the rhyme seems to falter (as it now does in some modern English accents):

MALCOLM
So thanks to all at once, and to each *one*,
Whom we invite to see us crowned at *Scone*.

One (pronounced like 'own') would have rhymed with *Scone* at the time Shakespeare was writing, but tends not to with some of the accents most commonly associated with Shakespeare performance over the last 100 years.

THOUGHTS VS SENTENCES

When looking at Shakespeare's writing it makes sense to think of the play as being full of speeches to be spoken out loud, rather than text to be read: we speak in thoughts; we write in sentences.

There are never absolute rules in Shakespeare, particularly for a time when punctuation and printing were far from being standardised, and there's often disagreement between different editors of Shakespeare's texts as to where the end of a thought may lie. For the purposes of this book, thoughts end in a full-stop, a question mark, or an exclamation mark. In the extracts used throughout, I'll mark where a thought ends by underlining the last few words.

A thought can finish at the end of a line of metre, like this:

LADY MACBETH
I heard the owl scream and the crickets cry.

When the end of a thought coincides with the end of a line of metre, it implies a calm, collected state of mind, contained by the poetic style. But a thought can also flow over many lines of metre – and end half-way through a metrical line. Take one of Macbeth's first speeches, when he meets the Witches for the first time:

MACBETH
Stay you imperfect speakers, tell me more.
By Sinel's death I know I am Thane of Glamis,
But how of Cawdor? The Thane of Cawdor lives
A prosperous man; and to be king
Stands not within the prospect of belief,
No more than to be Cawdor. Say from whence
You owe this strange intelligence, or why
Upon this blasted heath you stop our way
With such prophetic greeting? Speak, I charge you.

The notion here is that the thought is too big to be contained by the metre, perhaps indicating confusion or excitement, and so the character overwhelms the style, refusing to be contained by it. Shakespearean actors are encouraged to carefully give a rising intonation to their voice to make it clear, that while the metrical line has finished, the thought hasn't:

> By Sinel's death I know I am Thane of Glamis,
>   But <u>how of Cawdor?</u>

Delivering the metre in this way can make us think Macbeth has finished talking about the Thane, but instead carries on to talk about how he lives:

> The Thane of Cawdor lives
> A prosperous man...

If a part of a thought needs to be quoted, a / is used to show where the metrical line ends. So the line above would look like this: *The Thane of Cawdor lives / a prosperous man*

BREAKING DOWN A SPEECH

In the DURING section of the book, I've used some of the analytical tools actors use to help break open a character's speech, and begun to explore what might be happening in them.

Whatever the edition of the text you might be reading, a glance at the end of each thought can make for a quick reference guide to what the speech is about:

> Stay you imperfect speakers, <u>tell me more.</u>
> By Sinel's death I know I am Thane of Glamis,
> But <u>how of Cawdor?</u> The Thane of Cawdor lives
> A prosperous man; and to be king
> Stands not within the prospect of belief,
> No more than <u>to be Cawdor.</u> Say from whence
> You owe this strange intelligence, or why
> Upon this blasted heath you stop our way
> With <u>such prophetic greeting?</u> Speak, <u>I charge you.</u>

A quick count of

– how many lines a speech is made up of
– how many separate thoughts are within those lines
– how many of those thoughts end mid-line
– and how many of the thoughts are questions or exclamations

can equally give an idea as to what type of speech it is, and perhaps an insight into the character's state of mind. Characters who exclaim or ask questions are in a different state of mind from those who don't exclaim, and need no answer. Speeches with many thoughts indicate a mind moving quickly – perhaps less thoughtfully.

A speech full of longer thoughts indicate a mind more settled. A speech with many mid-line endings indicate a frantic, less composed state-of-mind – switching from subject to subject, the characters are interrupting themselves.

So, looking again at Macbeth's speech above:

– it's a 9 line speech
– which contains 5 thoughts
– 3 end mid-line
– and 2 are questions

From the questions and number of thoughts ending mid-line I know – without even looking at what Macbeth is *saying* – that he obviously wants more information about something, that he's slightly excited or troubled by something, but only slightly: his two middle thoughts are quite long, perhaps an indication he manages to retain some composure. Next to some of the speeches in the DURING section there might be a **+1** or **+2** next to a line. I'll explain what these mean in the AFTER section of the book, so ignore them for the time being.

SIDE-NOTE – *O*

Arguably, the most important word Shakespeare uses. The single letter *O* is the playwright asking the actor to express an emotion of some kind. But one that fits with the context of what is being said. Surprise, anger, frustration, love … the options are limitless.

SHARED LINES

When you're reading the play, you'll notice that a line sometimes begins half-way across the page, like this:

MACDUFF
                                        How does my wife?

The spacing indicates half a line of metre, known as a *shared line*. This is when one line of metre – or thought – is split or shared by two or more characters. Over the course of his career, Shakespeare made more and more of his characters speak in this way. They were not obviously laid out in print as shared lines until the 1780s, but this is the norm in modern editions.

By the time he wrote *Macbeth*, around a third of the lines in his plays were shared (compared to almost none in his earlier works). He realised that splitting the lines in this way makes for rapid-fire, pacy interaction, and *Macbeth* is the eighth largest play in the canon for shared lines. It's very much a play full of real dialogue, together with a number of isolated speeches.

In Act 1 Scene 7 (from here on I'll refer to particular scenes using numbers only, e.g. 1:7) Macbeth leaves a banquet he's holding for King Duncan, to think further about the bloody plan. Lady Macbeth enters, and he asks her if Duncan has noticed that he's left the feast:

MACBETH

1–5   Hath he asked for me?

LADY

6–10   Know you not he has?

The numbers to the left are the number of syllables, or beats, in each line of speech. Adding the two lines together makes ten syllables, and so a full line of metre.

Splitting the line of metre up between two characters means that in order to keep the rhythm bouncing along, Lady has to come in on her cue, with no pause after Macbeth has asked his question. It's a great writing effect, meant to bring pace and a sense of urgency to the dialogue.

MIND THE GAP

You'll notice that in the examples of verse above, there are ten syllables in each line. That should be true for every line of poetry written in this iambic pentameter form, and much of *Macbeth* is written in this way. When it changes (for example, when there are eight syllables, or two, or one in a line) *something* is going on in Shakespeare's writing.

In Act 3:4 Macbeth is at a feast with his generals and his wife. He suddenly sees Banquo's blood-covered ghost appear at the banqueting table, pointing at him:

MACBETH (to Banquo's ghost)

10   Thou canst not say I did it; never shake

1–6   Thy gory locks at me. (x \ x \)

ROSS

10   Gentlemen, rise. His highness is not well.

A gap in the metre (indicated by the grey tint and marking the missing beats) gives space for a movement or reaction of some kind.

Macbeth's first line and Ross's line both have ten syllables in them, as they should. Macbeth's second line only has six syllables, which means that in order to keep the iambic rhythm nice and steady, the actor playing Ross should wait a couple of beats before speaking.

It gives the actors on stage a moment to show the audience what they're thinking – a reaction shot – as they show surprise, or shock, or any number of emotions at their King's odd behaviour.

Later, as Ross prepares to deliver some terrible news to Macduff, a moment of hesitation has been written in on the 8th beat:

MACDUFF

                                    How does my wife?

ROSS

1–2   Why, well.

MACDUFF

3–7   And all my children?

ROSS

(8), 9–10   (x)Well too.

There are some fascinating gaps and changes in the metre in this play, and sometimes – and this just goes to show how good a dramatist Shakespeare was – it can be a space where the audience might laugh or gasp, or where characters can enter:

MACBETH

And Thane of Cawdor too, went it not so?

BANQUO

To th'selfsame tune and words.(x \ ) Who's here?

Enter Ross and Angus

Or a place for a sound effect:

LADY

My hands are of your colour; but I shame
To wear a heart so white.(x \ x \ )

Knock at the door

I hear a knocking at the south entry.

THOU AND YOU

This is an obscure point to modern eyes and ears, but it would have been so obvious to Shakespeare's audience it would almost be neon-lit.

In Shakespeare's time, English had two different ways of saying 'you', much like modern French. There was an informal *thou* (and its derivatives *thee*, *thy*, *thine* and *thyself*) and a formal *you* (and its derivatives *your*, *yours* and *yourself/ yourselves*). The distinction between these two forms was already breaking down in Shakespeare's London by the 1600s, but it seems he continued to use them as a fine dramatic device.

So whenever a character changes from one to another, it means something – perhaps a switch in attitude or a sudden flash of emotion. Considering why such a change happens (rather than dismissing it as a random or meaningless usage on Shakespeare's part) can often help open up a scene.

Typically, high-status characters would use *you* to each other, indicating a formal style of speech. *Thou* would be a marker of closeness – but a closeness that can mean anything from great intimacy to piercing insult.

In the relationship between Macbeth and Lady Macbeth, there's a sudden shift in the way they address each other:

> When he arrives back from battle, she shows both intimacy (*'Thy* letters have transported me…') and formality (*'Your* face my thane, is as a book…')

Two scenes later, when she realises he is reluctant to carry out their plan, everything changes:

> Lady Macbeth meets him outside the dining chamber, and addresses him more formally: 'Why have *you* left the chamber?'

As we'll see, after this scene she never refers to him using *thou* again…

ROSS, AND OTHER THANES

There's a famous saying in the acting world, that there are 'no small parts, only small actors', and that has been proved in some productions with the part of Ross.

One of the named Scottish Thanes (together with Menteth, Cathness, Angus and the young Lennox), he appears sporadically throughout the play at key moments. Productions have reinvented Ross as Macbeth's master spy, the man responsible for Banquo's and Lady Macduff's murder. He has also been reimagined as Duncan's priest, a man who bears witness to the tragic horror as they unfold and (taking on the role of Doctor) called on to minister to Lady Macbeth's sleep-walking.

Having been written in such an open-ended way, and not specified as being particularly good or bad, it's a part you can choose to do very little with and ignore or one that can be given an important narrative arc through the whole play.

THE WITCHES' SPEECH

The witches speak in short lines with four strong beats, a type of poetry called *trochaic tetrameter*, and you'll hear it in the opening lines of the play:

When shall **we**   three **meet**   a**gain**
DUM-de   **DUM**-de **DUM**-de **DUM**

In **thun**der   **light**ning **and**   in **rain**
de-**DUM** de-**DUM** de-**DUM** de-**DUM**

Shakespeare uses this rhythm of speech for the Faeries in *A Midsummer Night's Dream*, too. The rhythmical patterns can vary a little – notice that the first line begins by reversing the rhythm, with a **DUM**-de.

These *tetrameters* are a very subtle, but effective way of making the characters seem even more other-worldly than they would if Shakespeare had written their speeches in prose or regular iambic pentameter. These opening repeated four-beat lines convey a hypnotic sound that drums into our ears, and the effect is especially noticeable later in the play, when the witches concoct their spells.

THE FOURTH ACT

Having started out as an actor, Shakespeare not only shaped the metre to help his troupe perform his plays, but structured the entire play with an understanding of how actors work too. So he writes in a break for his tragic lead characters.

Around Act 4 in a Shakespearean tragedy, there'll be a run of scenes that don't feature the lead: whether it be Hamlet, King Lear or Macbeth, the lead character will disappear for a while, before returning for the final climactic scenes.

In *Macbeth*, Macbeth disappears after he has met the Witches for a second time, and doesn't reappear until six scenes later, much-changed and readying himself for battle. Most of the interim scenes are quite short, but there's one in particular between Macduff and Duncan's exiled son, Malcolm. Their discussion kick-starts the final act of the play, but, as we'll see, it's a long exchange, and can be problematic for actors and audience alike.

THE ENDING

At the end of recent productions of a Shakespeare play a dance, or jig, has been performed, where everyone – dead or alive, hero and villain – comes on-stage and dances.

It signifies the end of the play, bursting the bubble of the world they'd been in for the last few hours; a particularly important function after a tragedy like *Macbeth*, where the audience's emotions have been fairly wrung out. There's anecdotal evidence – again, from Swiss diarist Thomas Platter – that Shakespeare's Company did something similar to break the spell and bring everyone safely back into the real world.

The modern reconstructed Shakespeare's Globe – and others – have inserted similar dances before their final curtain call, and the catharsis that comes from this joint celebration can be exhilarating.

A WORD ON THE TEXT

Depending on which publisher's edition of the text has been used for the production, or which edition you're reading, the spellings – and indeed sometimes entire words or scenes – will appear differently.

The Hecate scenes (3:5 and 4:1) are now thought to have been written by Thomas Middleton, a collaborator who worked with Shakespeare towards the end of his career. Some productions include these scenes, some cut them.

Also, the editor of the Arden edition breaks up the scenes in Act 5 differ
ently from other editions, and has used elisions (such as *o'er* for *over*, and
bestow'd for *bestowed* to indicate when the verse requires two syllables to be
contracted into one), and made various editorial decisions (such as replacing
sennet for *sevennight*).

A FEW RELATIONSHIP / TITLE POINTS

Characters in Shakespeare plays often have a number of different names or
titles, and it isn't always clear how they relate to each other:

Macbeth – also referred to as (Thane* of) Glamis, later (Thane of) Cawdor
later King of Scotland; both he and Duncan and grandsons to the previous
King (Malcolm II) putting Macbeth next in line for the throne after Duncan's
sons

Macduff – also referred to as (Thane of) Fife

Malcolm – son of King Duncan, later Prince of Cumberland**, later King of
Scotland

Siward – Uncle to Malcolm, and so brother to King Duncan; Earl of
Northumberland, General of the English Army, living in England

*Thane – a person ranking with an earl's son, and holding lands of the king
Also used to refer to the chief of a clan, and one of the king's barons. Historical
titles are hard to relate to, but a Thane is similar to a Governor in Wild West
movies, helping reign over a section of the country for the President. Note that
at the end of the play the English-backed Malcolm abolishes this Scottish title
in favour of the English equivalent 'Earl'.

**Prince of Cumberland – The crown of Scotland was originally not hereditary
When a successor was declared in the lifetime of a king, the title of Prince of
Cumberland was immediately bestowed on him as the mark of his designation

CHARACTERS MENTIONED WHO DON'T APPEAR

Cawdor (Thane of) – a rebel against King Duncan. Duncan orders his
execution at the beginning of the play, and Macbeth is given his title – but
the opening scenes it can be confusing who the characters mean when they say
'Cawdor'

Macdonwald – a rebel against King Duncan, allying himself with the
Norwegians

Sweno – the King of Norway, fighting with the rebels Cawdor and Macdonwald

Sinel – Macbeth's father, once Thane of Glamis

LIST OF PROPS MENTIONED IN THE PLAY

(Assuming the male characters would originally already have hats, swords and / or daggers)

- a severed thumb
- daggers
- cauldron
- candle
- a drum
- boughs of trees

STAGE DIRECTIONS GLOSSARY

Each scene of the play in a modern text is preceded by a stage direction, introducing the characters, and often saying what is happening. When you go to see a theatre production, the director will have interpreted these directions for you. But if you're reading a text, you're likely to encounter the following terms:

alarum(s) = a call to arms

aside = in Shakespeare's time, a moment when the character speaks to the audience; in more modern times, sometimes spoken as a moment of internal reflection

colours = each army would have its own colours, shown on flags, shields and uniforms

divers = different, various, several

drum = a drum being beaten to signify an approaching army

exeunt = they exit (Latin plural of 'exit')

flourish = fanfare of horns or trumpets, usually accompanying an exit or entrance

hautboys = oboes playing, signalling entertainment being played off-stage

sennet = trumpet call signalling a procession

several [doors] = indicates characters enter from different points on the stage

sewer = chief servant, master of ceremonies

torch(es) = flaming torches to light the way (and in theatres like the Globe, to help signify night-time)

MAP OF LOCATIONS IN MACBETH

BIRNAM – a town in north-east Scotland; 15 miles from **Dunsinane**; the forest Malcolm uses to disguise his army is near here. In some editions of the text, spelt *Birnan*

CAWDOR – a town in the Highlands, north Scotland; Macbeth's new territory

COLMEKILL – Iona, an island off the west coast of Scotland; once the traditional burial place for Scottish kings – Duncan's body is taken there

DUNSINANE – Dunsinnan, a hill west of Dundee; site of the battle between (King) Macbeth and those rebellious to his monarchy, led by Malcolm, Macduff and the Earl of Northumberland; King Macbeth has a fortress near here

FIFE – a county north of Edinburgh, east Scotland; Macduff's territory

FORRES – a town and royal burgh in north Scotland; the battle between Duncan and Macdonwald takes place near here; King Duncan's (and later King Macbeth's) royal palace is here; the Witches' scenes are all set near here

GLAMIS – a town in east Scotland; Macbeth's territory

INVERNESS – northernmost city in the UK, north Scotland; the site of Macbeth's castle; 25 miles/about 3 hours' ride from **Forres**, where the opening battle is set

SAINT COLM'S INCH – Inchcolm, a small island in east Scotland; the site of an abbey, where the rebel Sweno must go to pay his tribute in order to gain permission to bury his dead soldiers; it's a long way from where the battle was – 145 miles, or about two days' ride south from Forres

SCONE – the ancient royal city, east Scotland; *The Stone of Destiny* lay here, on which Macbeth is crowned King

FINAL THOUGHTS

Before you head to the theatre, turn on the film, or open the book, it's worth-while to think about how the play you're about to experience might be staged. Would a big and varied set work best for this kind of play, or a bare stage? Should modern dress with guns be used, or costumes and weaponry from a particular period or event in history?

Macbeth is based on an eleventh-century Scottish story, but Shakespeare's actors wouldn't have performed it in Scottish accents – they weren't creating historical fiction-theatre – so it would be false to say it *should* be set somewhere in particular.

As with all theatre, the questions to ask are

- What does this play mean here, today, tonight?
- What makes people still want to produce it?
- And what does each character want from each scene?

These are the kinds of questions a production's rehearsal process begins with, and your own expectations of the answers will dramatically shape your experience of *Macbeth*...

If you want to sell out a theatre, just mount a production of Macbeth.
It's a short play, it's an exciting play, it's easy to understand, and it attracts great acting.

Sir Ian McKellen

DURING

FIVE INTERVAL WHISPERS

ACT 1
1:1 – The Witches

1 – 1:1 The Witches

Note the rhythm of their speech. Written in iambic tetrameter, a bea[t] short of the usual iambic pentameter. The drop of a beat will make the[m] sound odd and unnatural in comparison to other speakers. It's the first rhythm we hear, colouring the atmosphere of the play. The next rhythm we hear [is] iambic pentameter, spoken by King Duncan, but now *he's* the one who sound[s] unnatural.

1:2 – The Bloody Captain Scene
1:3 – Macbeth meets the Witches
1:4 – The honouring of Malcolm Scene
1:5 – Lady Macbeth's Letter Scene
1:6 – Duncan's arrival at Glamis Castle
1:7 – Macbeth's doubt and Lady Macbeth's persuasion

ACT 2
2:1 – The Floating Dagger Scene

2 – 2:1 'The Dagger Scene'

On his way to murder Duncan, Macbeth sees a dagger floating in the a[ir]

Is this a dagger, which I see before me
The handle toward my hand? Come, let me clutch thee:
I have thee not, and yet I see thee still…

When Shakespeare was writing the play the leading philosophers were tryi[ng] to establish whether it was possible to create physical matter by the power [of] the mind. It's a powerful moment: with the dagger floating before Macbet[h] Shakespeare was slamming the academic and theatrical worlds together. Th[is] in a building thought by many to be fit only for rogues and vagabonds.

---

3 – 2:3 The Porter

After the murder, and right before it's discovered, someone is knocking hard and loud at the castle gate, and the night-porter enters to answer it, still drunk after a night of celebrating. He stops on the way and talks to the audience. Pretending to be the gate-keeper to Hell, he imagines that different types of people who deserve to be in Hell are on the other side of the door.

He mentions an equivocator – someone who intentionally says one thing but means another, hiding their true meaning. Essentially, someone who deceives the person they're talking to. The idea of equivocation runs through the whole play, and the Porter subtly gives a spoiler for the ending.

2:4 – The Old Man Scene

ACT 3
3:1 – King Macbeth
3:2 – King and Lady Macbeth
3:3 – The Banquo and Fleance Scene
3:4 – The Banquet Scene
3:5 – The Hecat Scene

ACT 4
4:1 – **The Age of Kings / Prophecy Scene**

---

4 – 4:1 – The Prophecy Scene

Macbeth returns to the Witches. Now King, he wants to ensure he remains so:

The Witches show him three apparitions – an armed head, a bloody child, and a crowned child with a tree in its hand:

– The first tells him to beware of Macduff, the Thane of Fife
– The second tells him he needs to fear no man born of woman
– The third that Macbeth will remain King until the wood in Birnam comes to Dunsinane Hill

Macbeth then asks about Banquo's children becoming king, and a line of eight kings appear, followed by an image of Banquo. This was a politic move on Shakespeare's part – the eighth king would be seen as King James VI, the relatively new monarch of England when the play was written, who was actually a descendent of the real Banquo.

The 'two-fold balls' which the eighth king carries is thought to be a reference to James' double coronation at Westminster and at Scone. In a command performance at court, the actors might well have gestured towards this real descendent of Banquo, sitting in their audience.

4:2 – The Macduff Family Scene
4:3 – **The Malcolm Scene**

5 – 4:3 – The Malcolm and Macduff Scene

The scene opens with a relatively long (114 line) dialogue as Malcolm pretends he has none of the attributes befitting a monarch, before finally revealing his true allegiance and character. Malcolm presents himself to Macduff as a sort of super-pure, asexual man – what does it mean that this figure intends to end the reign of the Macbeths, the couple with one of the most powerfully dramatised marriages in English theatre?

The scene does slow the pace of the play down, but it equally shows how far Macbeth's power has reached through his network of spies, making everyone suspicious of everyone else. What's more, the end of the scene brings shocking dramatic news.

ACT 5
5:1 – The Sleepwalking Scene
5:2 – The Scottish Rebels' Scene
5:3 – 5:7 – The Battle scenes

Act 1:1

Location: *Unspecified*

Characters: *Three Witches*

Action: *One of the most famous scenes in the canon. We see three Witches at the end of a gathering, discussing the next time they'll meet each other: it will be on a heath once the nearby battle (between the Kings Duncan and Sweno) is over.*

They foresee that they will meet Macbeth. As they leave, the Witches dance and chant – as Shakespeare's audience believed witches did at the end of a meeting.

☞ NAMES   THE WITCHES' FAMILIARS

People believed a Witch could be easily spotted because a familiar spirit (or simply a **familiar** = a close companion) would never be too far away. Usually animals, they were understood to be supernatural figures able to assist in the practice of Magicke, and would protect a young Witch as she begins to use her powers.

As the Witches leave, they call to their familiars:

> The First Witch calls out to **Graymalkin** = a grey cat
> The Second Witch calls to **Paddock** = a toad
> The Third Witch doesn't name her familiar*, but says **'Anon'** = soon, as if in response to an unheard call – 'I'm coming soon'

*we discover in 4:1 that the Third Witch's familiar is a **Harpier** = an owl or a harpy, a mythical bird, half woman-half vulture

☞ RHYME   THE WITCHES

The Weird Sisters somehow foresee their meeting with Macbeth:

> Where the place? / Upon the heath / There to meet with Macbeth

Coming after the opening rhyming lines **again/rain done/ won/sun**, some productions have played the **Macbeth / heath** lines as a failed rhyme – one of the Witches comically getting it wrong. The vowel sounds have changed over the last four centuries; in Shakespeare's time *heath* would have rhymed with *Macbeth*.

☞ SIDE-NOTE   THE WITCHES' EXIT

Their exiting rhyming couplet runs:

> Fair **is** foul, **and** foul is **fair:**
> **H**over **through** the **fog** and **fil**thy **air**

The first line has three strong beats, the second has five strong beats, which is more like the verse we expect to hear in a Shakespeare play (see BEFORE, p.10). But it's a nine-syllable line (rather than ten), making a bridge from the Witches' tetrameter to Duncan's pentameter which opens the next scene, with the possible effect of their chant blending and shifting into regular speech.

Act 1:2

Location: *A military camp near Forres, on the coast of northern Scotland*

Characters (in order of appearance): *King Duncan, Malcolm, Donalbain, Lennox, Attendants, Captain, Ross, Angus*

☞ WORDS

• *what **bloody** man is that?* = wounded in the battle; the word *blood* or *bloody* is mentioned over 40 times in the play

• *Till that **Bellona's** bridegroom* = the Roman goddess of war: Macbeth is described as her husband, implying he has awesome fighting skills

• *they meant to… memorise another **Golgotha*** – literally 'the place of skulls'; in the Bible, the place where Jesus was crucified; in other words, as if 'Banquo and Macbeth fought as if they meant to produce another memorable skull-strewn site of death'

🗣 **SPEECH**   THE CAPTAIN

A speech of 17 lines, 3 thoughts, 2 ending mid-line. Note how his thoughts end mid-line, and break the metre. Also a gap in the metre, towards the end – as he gasps for breath, struggling to relate the story to his King?

The bloody Captain's description of the battle he has survived is a famous speech; dramatically it's important as it includes our first image of Macbeth. The Captain saw him fight unbelievably bravely and ferociously:

CAPTAIN

                              Doubtful it stood;
As two spent swimmers, that do cling together   +1
And <u>choke their art.</u> The merciless **Macdonwald**   +1
(Worthy to be a rebel, for to that
The multiplying villainies of nature
Do swarm upon him) from the Western Isles

Macdonwald – Rebel to King Duncan, ally to the Norwegian King Sweno

31

Of **Kerns** and **Gallowglasses** is supplied;
And **Fortune,** on his damned quarrel smiling   +1
Showed like <u>a rebel's whore.</u> But all's too weak:
For brave Macbeth (well he deserves that name)
Disdaining Fortune, with his brandish'd steel,
Which smok'd with bloody execution,
Like Valour's minion, carv'd out his passage
Till he fac'd the slave; (x \ x \ x)   -5
Which ne'er shook hands nor bade farewell to him
Till he **unseam'd** him from the nave to th'chops,
And fix'd his head <u>upon our battlements.</u>

kerns = Irish
mercenaries fighting
with the rebel
Macdonwald; Macbeth
later hires them for his
battle against Malcolm

gallowglasses =
horsemen armed with
axes, fighting with the
rebel Macdonwald

Fortune – depicted as
a blindfolded woman,
on a moving wheel

unseam'd – split from
navel to jaws with his
sword

....

☞ SIDE-NOTE   10,000 DOLLARS

The *dollar* or *thaler* was a German silver coin, varying in value
from country to country, but in England was worth about 60
pence. The charge placed against the Norwegian King Sweno
to allow him the right to bury his dead after defeat is a vast
10,000 dollars (equivalent to £250,000 today):

ROSS
Nor would we deign him burial of his men
Till he disbursed at **St Colme's Inch**
Ten thousand Dollars to our general use.

St Colme's Inch – the
site of an abbey 145
miles away, where
Sweno must deliver
his tribute of 10,000
dollars. See Map (p.22)

Act 1:3

Location: *A heath near Forres*

Characters: *Three Witches, Macbeth, Banquo, Ross, Angus*

Action: *The witches chant, relating to each other where
they've been since they saw each other last. They hear a drum
beating – the sound of soldiers approaching – and somehow
already know that Macbeth and Banquo are near, victorious
from battle and returning to Duncan's camp.*

The witches prophesy that Macbeth will become Thane of Cawdor, and King of Scotland. After being entreated by Banquo, the witches then prophesy that he will be a father of kings, though he won't be one himself. The noblemen Ross and Angus arrive, and give Macbeth his new title – the Thane of Cawdor – and the witches' recent fantastical prophecies suddenly seem all the more real.

○ SPEECH   THE FIRST WITCH

The First Witch does most of the talking, the others reinforcing her. Her description of where she's been and what she's done gives an idea of their very real influence and power:

FIRST WITCH
A sailor's wife had chestnuts in her lap,
And **mounch'd**, and mounchd, and mounch'd: 'Give me' quoth I:
'**Aroint** thee Witch!' the rump-fed **ronyon** cries.
Her husband's to **Aleppo** gone, **master'o'th'Tiger:**
But in a sieve I'll thither sail
And like a rat without a tail;
I'll do, I'll do, I'll do.

mounch'd = munched, ate heartily
Aroint = Get away!
ronyon = mangy creature
Aleppo – the largest city in Syria, famous for its military proficiency; an incredible distance to travel to
Tiger – before Macbeth was first performed a ship called the Tiger had just returned from a voyage where the Master of the Ship had been killed
I'll do – the Witch is going to somehow take revenge on the Sailor

☞ NAMES

• *by Sinel's death I know I am Thane of Glamis* – Sinel was Macbeth's father; his title automatically passed to his son when he died, making Macbeth the Thane of Glamis; it's possible Sinel was fighting in the recent battle

☞ WORDS

• *the shipman's card* = a compass-card, on which the 32 points of the compass are marked
• The **Weird** Sisters = *weird* here carries the notion of *fateful* rather than the modern sense of *odd-looking*; sometimes spelt *weyrd/weyward*; the similar-sounding Wyrd was Anglo-Saxon for *Fate*

- *for an **earnest** of a greater honour* = a pledge, payment in advance
- ***blasted** heath* = *blighted, withered, rather than an expression of dislike*; the evil of the witches is reflected in the grim landscape, perhaps a state caused by their being there

Act 1:4

Location: *Unspecified; possibly the military camp near Forres; or The Royal Palace near Forres*

Characters: *King Duncan, Lennox, Malcolm, Donalbain, Attendants, Macbeth, Banquo, Ross, and Angus*

Action: *Some productions imply a time-shift between this scene and the previous. Macbeth and Banquo are warmly welcomed by King Duncan. Duncan honours their success in battle, but proclaims Malcolm as his heir to the throne, and announces that the celebratory feast will be held at Macbeth's castle in Inverness. Coming directly after the Witches' prophecies, this scene immediately places an obstacle between Macbeth and the crown.*

◯ SPEECH DUNCAN

The King moves from no trust to absolute trust. In discussing his relationship with Cawdor as Macbeth enters, he unknowingly describes his future relationship with Macbeth:

DUNCAN
                There's no art
To find the mind's construction <u>in the face.</u>
He was a gentleman on whom I built
An absolute trust –
Enter Macbeth, Banquo, Ross and Angus

           O worthiest cousin!

💬 SPEECH DUNCAN

The King announces who will be heir to this throne. Does the audience see a reaction from Macbeth at this point?:

DUNCAN

                My plenteous joys,
Wanton in fulness, seek to hide themselves
In drops <u>of sorrow</u>. Sons, kinsmen, Thanes,
And you whose places are the nearest, know
We will establish our estate upon*
Our eldest, Malcolm; whom we name hereafter   +1
The Prince of Cumberland: which honour must
Not unaccompanied invest him only,
But signs of nobleness, like stars, shall shine
On <u>all deservers</u>. From hence to **Inverness**,   +1
And bind us <u>further to you</u>. (\ x \ )   -3

– no metrical gap, but often a pause here as Duncan hesitates, and Macbeth reacts, expecting to be made heir?

The Prince of Cumberland *– Malcolm is designated the heir to the crown. see BEFORE (p.20)*

Inverness *– Macbeth's castle; about three hours away by horse*

💬 SPEECH MACBETH

Macbeth talks to the audience after Duncan's announcement. The news might have turned Macbeth away from his darker thoughts; on the contrary, it seems to have reinforced them:

MACBETH

The Prince of Cumberland – that is a step
On which I must fall down, or else o'er leap,
For **in my** <u>way it lies.</u> Stars, <u>hide your fires!</u>
Let not light see my black and deep desires...

in my way it lies – a scene ago, Macbeth considered Chance may make him King. Duncan is to stay at his castle; at what point does Macbeth see the opportunity for murder?

....

🖙 WORDS

I'll be myself the **harbinger** = forerunner, precursor, herald; often of bad news

Act 1:5

Location: *Macbeth's castle, Inverness*

Characters: *Lady Macbeth, Messenger, Macbeth*

Action: *Lady Macbeth enters reading out loud a letter from Macbeth, which tells of his encounter with the witches.*

As a result, we're introduced to a new lead character in the play and at the same time see how she reacts to information we already know: the contents of the letter are less important than Lady's reactions to them.

Every production has a different take on what kind of physical or sexual relationship Macbeth and Lady have when they first meet and how they greet each other, as it sets up their relationship for the rest of the play. The chemistry – or lack thereof – between the two actors in this scene usually dominates the post-theatrical discussion (see AFTER pp.80–1).

◯ SPEECH LADY MACBETH

Lady reads her husband's letter, written in prose, and her reactions hint at the impending conflict between them, though (at this point) there does seem to be a strong but loving side to her.

Her speech in verse (16 lines, 4 thoughts, all end mid-line) following the letter begins erratically (indicated by the metrical overflow), tallying with her excitement, then becomes increasingly metrically regular, as she takes control of her thoughts. It appears we meet Lady Macbeth as she is halfway through reading the letter:

LADY

*'They met me in the **day of success**, and I have learn'd by the **perfect'st report**, they have more in them than mortal knowledge. When I burn'd in desire to question them further, they made themselves air, into which they vanish'd. Whiles I stood rapt in the wonder of it, came missives from the King, who all-hail'd me 'Thane of Cawdor'; by which title before these Weird Sisters saluted me, and referred me to the coming on of time with, 'Hail, king that shalt be.' This have I thought good to deliver thee, my dearest partner of greatness, that thou mightest not lose the dues of rejoicing by being ignorant of what greatness is promised thee. Lay it to thy heart, and farewell.'*

Glamis thou art, and Cawdor, and shalt be (x)	-1
What <u>thou art promis'd.</u> Yet do I fear thy nature:	+2
It is too full o'th' **milk of human-kindness**	+1
To catch <u>the **nearest** way.</u> Thou wouldst be great;	
Art not without ambition, but without	
The **illness** should attend it; what thou wouldst	
highly	+2
That wouldst thou **holily**; wouldst not play false,	
And yet wouldst wrongly win; thou'dst have, great Glamis,	
That which cries, 'Thus thou must do,' if thou have it;	+1
And that which rather thou dost fear to do,	
Than wishest <u>should be undone.</u> Hie thee hither,	+1
That I may pour my spirits in thine ear,	
And chastise with the valour of my tongue	
All that impedes thee from the **golden round**,	
Which fate and metaphysical aid doth seem	
To have <u>thee crown'd withal.</u>	

day of success – the day they defeated the Norwegians and rebelling Scots

perfect'st report – accurate information

Glamis – Lady speaks as if Macbeth were there.

(x) – as she takes a breath before speaking the idea out loud?

milk of human-kindness = gentle, weak; now a famous phrase in modern English

nearest = most direct

illness = evil

highly … holily = wanting to achieve greatness honestly

golden round = the crown

The relationship between Macbeth and Lady Macbeth is … obsession … he has completely sold his soul to her

Sir Patrick Stewart, 2008

💬 SPEECH LADY MACBETH

Lady calls on the spirits of night and darkness to ready herself for what she is planning. A speech of 16 lines, 5 thoughts, all end mid-line, indicating excitement, but generally much more metrically regular.

Few other female characters in Shakespeare equal her ferocity of thought at this moment, in a passage often referred to as the *Unsex me now* speech. *Unsex me* means *remove my femininity* (a quality associated with kindness), and the phrase is a powerful (and characteristically Shakespearean) coinage:

LADY

        The raven himself is hoarse,
That croaks the fatal entrance of Duncan
Under <u>my battlements.</u> Come, you Spirits
That tend on mortal thoughts, unsex me here,
And fill me from the **crown** to the toe top-full   +1
Of <u>direst cruelty.</u> Make thick my blood,
Stop up th'access and passage to remorse;
That no **compunctious** visitings of nature   +1
Shake my fell purpose, nor keep peace between
<u>Th'effect and it.</u> Come to my woman's breasts
And take my milk for **gall**, you **murth'ring**
   ministers,   +1
Wherever, in your sightless substances,
You wait on <u>nature's mischief.</u> Come, thick Night,
And pall thee in the **dunnest** smoke of Hell,
That my keen knife see not the wound it makes,
Nor heaven peep through the blanket of the dark
To <u>cry,</u> '**Hold**, hold!'

crown = head; also a play on 'royal crown'

compunctious = remorseful; only use of this word in Shakespeare

gall = bile; turn life-nourishment to something bitter tasting

murth'ring = murdering; the *th* was standard pronunciation at the time

dunnest = darkest

Hold – make the nigh so dark not even Heaven can see to shout Stop

38

Act 1:6

Location: *Outside Macbeth's castle, Inverness*

Characters: *King Duncan, Malcolm, Donalbain, Banquo, Lennox, Macduff, Ross, Angus, Attendants, Lady Macbeth*

Action: *Inverness is 25 miles (2-3 hours' ride) from the battleground in Forres, and Macbeth has ridden fast to get there before the King and his generals. The scene, beginning with Duncan's pleasant description, has something of the 'calm before the storm' about it.*

The stage direction notes torches, *indicating Duncan and his Thanes have arrived late in the day*

💬 SPEECH DUNCAN

Considering what we know about the Macbeths' plans for him, it's a little ironic that the scene starts with Duncan describing of their castle as being well-positioned, with a good atmosphere:

DUNCAN
This castle hath a pleasant seat; the air
Nimbly and sweetly recommends itself
Unto our gentle senses.

💬 SPEECH LADY MACBETH

Lady's speeches to Duncan seem overly flowery, complicated answers. Are they over-enthusiastic attempts at sincerity, nervousness at being in the presence of royalty, or something else?:

LADY

                            Your servants ever
Have theirs, themselves, and what is theirs, **in compt,**
To make their audit at your Higness' pleasure,
Still to **return your own.**

....

☞ WORDS

• *Herein I teach you / How you shall bid* **God'ild** *us for your pains* = a form of 'God yield', reward, repay, requite; a wish full of irony, in view of later events

• *had a purpose/To be his* **purveyor** = they had intended to be at the castle before Macbeth, and prepare for him

Act 1:7

Location: *Macbeth's castle, Inverness*

Characters: *Sewer, Servants, Macbeth, Lady Macbeth*

Action: *A few hours later. The scene begins outside a banquet room in Macbeth's castle. The Sewer* and servants imply a ceremonial air; an orderly dinner party for Duncan, compared to the later disorderly banquet in 3:4.*

*The Sewer was the Chief Servant who tasted dishes for the King to ensure they were not poisoned; an ominous sign and a lovely small detail in the stage directions at this point in the play

○ SPEECH   MACBETH 28-lines; 5 thoughts, all mid-line endings; no questions.

Macbeth wrestles with the idea of murdering Duncan. As he comes to the end of talking the issue out, the verse settles down, and becomes more regular – as he comes to making a decision?

As in Lady Macbeth's speech in 1:5, all the thoughts end halfway through the line of poetry, indicating a less-composed state of mind as Macbeth interrupts himself, or doesn't completely finish speaking out each idea. He keeps using the pronoun 'we' not 'I'. Is he already adopting the royal 'we'? Or extending his moral dilemma to include the audience? Note his final thought is interrupted by Lady's entrance:

MACBETH

If **it** were done when 'tis done, then 'twere well
It were done quickly: if th' Assassination   **+1**
Could trammel up the consequence, and catch
With his surcease, success; that but this blow
Might be the **be-all** and the end-all – here,
But here, upon this bank and shoal of time,
We'd jump the <u>life to come.</u> But in these cases   **+1**
We still have judgement here; that we but teach
Bloody instructions, which, being taught, return   **+1**
To plague th'inventor: this even-handed justice   **+2**
Commends th'ingredience of our poisoned Chalice   **+1**
To <u>our own lips.</u> He's here in double trust,   **+1**
First, as I am his kinsman and his subject,   **+1**
Strong both against the deed; then, as his host,
Who should against his murderer shut the door,
Not bear the <u>knife myself.</u> Besides, this Duncan   **+1**
Hath **borne his faculties so meek**, hath been
So clear in his great office, that **his virtues**   **+1**
Will plead like angels, trumpet-tongu'd against
The deep damnation of his **taking-off;**
And Pity, like a naked new-born babe
Striding the blast, or heaven's Cherubins, hors'd   **+1**
Upon the sightless couriers of the air,
Shall blow the horrid deed in every eye,
That tears shall <u>drown the wind.</u> I have **no spur**
To prick the sides of my intent but only   **+1**
Vaulting ambition which o'erleaps itself
And falls <u>on th'other-</u>

Enter Lady Macbeth
                How now? What news?

it – he doesn't – or can't – use the word `murder'

be-all and the end-all – naive hope, that he can easily get away with murdering the King; now a common phrase in English

borne his faculties so meek – Duncan has used his powers carefully

his virtues / will plead like angels – on Judgement Day, in the Court of Heaven

taking-off = euphemism for murder; Macbeth still avoids using the word

no spur – the ferocious language and persuasion from his wife restores his resolve – it is her plot, after all

vaulting ambition – terrific image; in its eagerness, 'ambition' makes the leap to success, but stumbles and falls

41

☞ WORDS

- *trammel* up = entangle, catch
- *as I am his* **kinsman** = member of the same race or tribe
- *striding the* **blast** = the storm of grief
- **sightless** *couriers* = invisible
- *heaven's* **Cherubins** = plural of *Cherubim*, one of the highest ranks in the hierarchy of angels

☞ THOU / YOU

Macbeth suggests to Lady Macbeth that they shouldn't continue with their plan to kill Duncan. She manages to persuade him that they should, but from this moment on she never calls him *thou* again, only referring to him as *you*.

The modern equivalent would be never calling your husband *love*, or *sweetheart* ever again. It's a subtle switch, but a huge moment in their relationship. See BEFORE (pp. 17–18).

☞ SIDE-NOTE 'WE FAIL?' VS 'WE FAIL!'

Macbeth asks his wife what might happen *If we should fail?* in their plot to murder the King (the answer is a traitors' death for both of them). In most modern editions of the play, Lady M replies:

> We fail!

In the First Folio text she replies:

> We fail?

pointing towards a very different type of response: the first is some sort of exclamation, the second, a question. The debate over which fits best has made for great theatrical and academic discussion.

Act 2:1

Location: *The court of Macbeth's castle, Inverness*

Characters: *Banquo, Fleance, Macbeth, Servant*

Action: *Banquo and his son Fleance are keeping watch outside the castle. It's after midnight and no moon is visible, so Fleance is lighting their way with a flaming torch. They encounter Macbeth (on his way to kill Duncan), and Banquo gives a* **diamond** *from the King, a gift in thanks for the good hospitality – a fitting, symbolic last chance for Macbeth to change his mind?*

The discussion of the Witches between Macbeth and Banquo brings a heavy contrast between them as they discuss the prophecies: the lying, plotting Macbeth (I think not of them), and the loyal, moral Banquo (my bosom franchised, my allegiance clear). It's a dangerous conversation – even talking about what the Witches told them is tantamount to treason.

Although he says little in the scene, this is our first introduction to Fleance, an important figure in the Witches' prophecies (see AFTER pp.77–98).

diamond – an ironic gift, in the eyes of Shakespeare's audience – a diamond was thought to protect the owner from witchcraft

....

☞ WORDS

• *sent forth great* **largess** *to your* **offices** = gifts of money, servants quarters
• **shut up** */ In measureless content* = finish the day
• *my bosom* **franchised** = free from guilt

💬 SPEECH MACBETH

34 lines; 17 thoughts, 8 mid-line endings; 3 questions, 1 exclamation. A balance of metrically regular and irregular lines at the beginning, with three questions and the exclamation, indicating a state of confusion; with a number of shorter thoughts ending with the metrical line, as he struggles to keep calm?

On his way to murder Duncan, Macbeth sees a dagger floating in the air that he can't grasp hold of. It's the most famous speech in the play, and after the earlier magic-realism of the Witches appearing and disappearing, we now see a character convinced of another apparition on-stage, that we may not be able to see.

It's a powerful dramatic conceit, reinforcing the supernatural ideas running through the play. Macbeth mentions witchcraft in the speech, so the weird sisters seem to be very much on his mind. Indeed, some productions have had the Witches on-stage (but invisible to Macbeth), holding the dagger in front of him. See After (p.90):

MACBETH
Go bid thy mistress, when my drink is ready
She strike <u>upon the bell.</u> Get <u>thee to bed.</u>

Exit Servant

Is this a dagger which I see before me,	+1
The handle <u>toward my hand?</u> Come, let me clutch thee –	+2
I have thee not and yet I <u>see thee still!</u>	
Art thou not, fatal vision, **sensible**	
To feeling <u>as to sight?</u> Or art thou but	
A dagger of the mind, a false creation,	+1
Proceeding from the <u>heat-oppressed brain?</u>	
I see thee yet, in form as palpable	
As this which <u>now I draw.</u>(x \ x \ )	
Thou marshall'st me the way that I was going,	+1
And such an instrument I <u>was to use.</u> –	
Mine eyes are made the fools o'th'other senses,	+1
Or else worth all the rest: I see thee still;	
And, on thy blade and dudgeon, gouts of blood,	
Which was <u>not so before.</u> There's <u>no such thing</u>.	+1
It is the bloody business which informs	
Thus <u>to mine eyes.</u> Now o'er the one half-world	
Nature seems dead, and wicked dreams abuse	
<u>The curtained sleep.</u> Witchcraft celebrates	
Pale **Hecate's** offerings; and wither'd Murther,	+1
Alarum'd by his sentinel the **wolf**,	

is – it a dagger? Is it real? Or is it my imagination?

sensible = perceptibl? to feeling, tangible

**X ** – Macbeth draws his own dagger? compares them both or as he follows the floating dagger?

Hecate – the Greek Goddess of the Underworld / the Witches' Mistress; he offerings (rituals) take place at night; she appears in 3:5

wolf – associated wi? murder; the classica? tale of Lyacon, a murderer who was turned into a wolf i? punishment

Whose howl's his watch, thus with his stealthy pace,
With **Tarquin**'s ravishing strides, towards his design+1
Moves <u>like a ghost.</u> Thou sure and firm-set earth,
Hear not my steps, which way they walk, for fear
Thy very stones prate of my where-about
And take the present horror from the time
Which now <u>suits with it.</u> – Whiles I threat, he **lives**:
Words to the heat of deeds too cold <u>breath</u> **gives.**

A bell rings

I go, and it is done; **the <u>bell</u> invites me.**   +1
Hear it not, Duncan, for it is a knell
That summons thee to heaven <u>or to hell.</u>

Exit

Tarquin – *Tarquinus Sextus; ravished (raped) Lucretia at night; does Macbeth notice his own lust to kill? has his physicality changed, the way he walks?*

Lives / gives – *rhyming couplet, as he prepares to leave. Talking about murdering Duncan does nothing*

bell – *Lady Macbeth has rung the bell; Macbeth hears the sound as an invitation; also a bell of doom: a death-knell (bells were rung for marriages and deaths) for Duncan – and for Macbeth!*

☞ WORDS

- *thou* **marshall'st** *me* = direct
- *thy blade and* **dudgeon** = the handle, or hilt of a dagger
- *Pale* **Hecate's** *offering* = Greek Goddess of the Underworld/ the Witches mistress; her offerings (rituals) take place at night; she appears in 3:5
- *towards his* **design** = intention, purpose

Act 2:2

Location: *Macbeth's castle, Inverness*

Characters: *Lady Macbeth, Macbeth*

Action: *Lady Macbeth waits as her husband murders the King in their house. It's an incredibly dramatic, tense scene and one of my favourites: every sound could be someone waking up to discover them with blood on their hands. If they succeed they are King and Queen. If they are discovered, they will be tried and killed for high treason.*

Note Macbeth's final line in the scene – Wake Duncan with thy knocking. I would thou couldst. – does he really already wish the deed undone?

💬 SPEECH LADY MACBETH

As Lady waits for her husband to return from killing Duncan, she tells us the part she played: having drugged the King's guards, and they fallen asleep, she took their daggers and placed them ready for her husband near the sleeping King. She tells us that if Duncan had not looked like her father, she would have killed him herself:

LADY

> Had he not resembled
> My father as he slept, I had **don't.**(x)

don't – rather than done it: gap in the metre, allowing a (very) short pause to show the audience how she feels about this fatherly image

Why would she murder Duncan, when she knows she has persuaded Macbeth to do it? And what psychological horrors lie in wait for her if she sees her father in the man they murder?

Lady Macbeth returns the daggers to the King's chamber; in so doing, covering her hands in blood, and momentarily sees the image she did not want to see – an image of her 'father' murdered. As we'll see, both these images have a tremendous effect on her state of mind later in the play.

💬 SPEECH MACBETH

Macbeth asks if she heard anything while he was murdering the King, Lady Macbeth replies, and then the verse is broken up into fragmented dialogue.

The gaps written into the metre orchestrate the dramatic pacing of the scene, creating a tension between them and everything off-stage that they're listening out for. Note how one line of metre is split into four conversational turns between two people – they respond to each other immediately, jumping on each other's words:

LADY
I heard the **owl** scream, and the **crickets cry**.
Did not you speak?

MACBETH
                    When?

LADY
                              Now.

MACBETH
                                        As I descended?

LADY
Ay. (x \ x \ x \ x \ x)

MACBETH
Hark. (x \ x \ x \ x \ x)
Who lies i'th'second chamber?

LADY
                                        Donalbain.*

MACBETH
This is a sorry sight. (x \ x \ )

LADY
A foolish thought, to say a sorry sight.

owl – the sound of an owl screaming was a very bad omen

crickets cry – the initial sounds cr, cr, making the noise of crickets at night

x \ – after machine-gun fast dialogue, the first of two long silences – as they try to hear if anyone has woken up?

hark = listen! – Macbeth thinks he hears something

*no gap in the metre; Lady needs no time to think before responding; she knows the answer – she has planned the murder well

x \ – as Macbeth takes in the situation between them? or as Lady reacts in disbelief at her husband's foolishness?

....

☞ WORDS

• *I have drugged their* **possets** = a restorative hot drink, made of milk, liquor and other ingredients; she has given them a supposedly innocent drink that should keep them awake, but added something that will make them sleep instead

• *this my hand will rather / The multitudinous seas* **incarnadine** = turn blood-red in colour; he sees so much blood that it would make all the seas in the world turn from green to red as the blood spread through them; one of the most vivid images – and famous lines – in the play

Act 2:3

Location: *Macbeth's castle, Inverness*

Characters: *Porter, Macduff, Lennox, Macbeth, Lady Macbeth, Banquo, Malcolm, Donalbain*

Action: *The night-porter opens the door to Macduff and Lennox, who have come to escort the King from the castle. Macduff is led to the King's chamber by Macbeth, discovers the murder, and wakes the other sleepers while Macbeth kills the King's guards to cover his tracks. The King's sons, Malcolm and Donalbain, concerned that the others suspect them for the murder – or that the murderer could be planning their deaths next – flee to England and Ireland.*

At any point during this scene, Macbeth and Lady Macbeth could be found out and would sorely pay for the consequences – they are likely to be highly strung on the inside, while the picture of surprise, shock and grief on the outside; the perfect double-act.

Fortunately for them, the Thanes are dealing with having seen the bloodied and dead body of their King. As they dispute with each other, Malcolm, the heir to the throne, realises the finger of blame could point towards him or his brother.

Ross is not named in this scene, but depending on how he's played, in some productions he's on-stage with the other Thanes, to watch and listen.

$\bigcirc$ SPEECH THE PORTER

A tricky speech; there's a longer discussion of the Porter in BEFORE (pp.9–10) and in AFTER (pp.90–1).

The night-porter, still drunk or hungover from the night's celebrations, comes to answer the door, but pretends to the audience he's the porter to the gate of Hell.

He imagines three different people who deserve to go to Hell are waiting to be let in, and jokes about them.

Some of the jokes have a 400-year-old sociological reference underpinning them, so are not easy to understand; on the other hand, he's essentially playing the *Knock knock! Who's there?* joke with the audience. Most importantly, he jokes about an *equivocator* — someone who intentionally deceives the person they're talking to:

Enter a Porter. Knocking within
PORTER
Here's a knocking indeed! If a man were porter of Hell Gate, he should have **old** turning the key.

Knock

Knock, knock, knock. Who's there i'th' name of **Belzebub**? Here's a **farmer** that hang'd himself on th' expectation of plenty. Come in time-pleaser; Have napkins **enow** about you; here you'll sweat for't.

Knock

Knock, knock. Who's there **i'th'other** devil's name? Faith, here's an **equivocator**, that could swear in both the **scales** against either scale; who committed treason enough for God's sake, yet could not equivocate to heaven: O, come in, equivocator.

Knock

Knock, knock, knock. Who's there? Faith, here's an English tailor come hither for stealing out of a **French hose:** come in, tailor; here you may roast your **goose.**

Knock

Knock, knock. Never at quiet! What are you? – But this place is too cold for hell. I'll devil-porter it no further: I had thought to have let in some of all professions that go the **primrose way** to th'everlasting bonfire.

Knock

Anon, anon: I pray you remember the Porter.

He opens the gate. Enter Macduff and Lennox.

old – plenty of turns of the key

Beelzebub – a name for the Devil

farmer – saved his crops hoping to sell them at a higher price the following year. prices fell, so he killed himself

enow – enough

i'th'other – the Porter has forgotten, or is reluctant to mention the other name for the Devil?

equivocator...
scales – the scales of justice; someone who lies under oath at trial

French hose – English trousers were fashionably baggy, so tailors could steal cloth from them. The French style was tighter, so the tailor's deception was noticed

goose = heat your iron (to smooth out wrinkles in clothes)

primrose way – the flowery way; the path to Hell, but at least, the way is pretty

Anon = `I'm coming' – to the people knocking; or `more later' – to the audience

49

☞ WORDS

• *destroy your sight / With a new* **Gorgon** = in classical mythology, one of three monster sisters, with eyes that could turn people to stone; the shock of seeing the murdered King will almost turn them to stone

Act 2:4

Location: *Outside Macbeth's castle, Inverness*

Characters: *Ross, Old Man, Macduff*

Action: *This scene is sometimes cut from productions, but coming immediately after the discovery of Duncan's murder, it's an important one.*

The two men talk of day seeming like night, and of the King's horses eating each other. They talk of a world that has turned upside down, that has become most 'unnatural': as far as Shakespeare's audience was concerned, if a monarch died and was replaced by the wrong heir, that would be reflected in Nature.

Towards the end of the scene Macduff enters, on his way home to Fife, and confirms Macbeth's earlier hopes: suspicion of the King's murder has landed on Duncan's servants and his two sons.

The country is in turmoil, but Macbeth is about to be crowned King, and has managed to shift blame for the murder. Dramatically, it's another moment of calm before the storm, and as such, it's often the final scene before the interval in a theatre production.

....

☞ CHARACTER The OLD MAN

The character of the Old Man is like a classic theatrical Chorus figure, seeing and reflecting on events that have taken place outside the world of the castle. His age (*three score and ten* = 70 years; it was also a phrase from the Bible, meaning 'the entire span of life') would have seemed terribly old to Shakespeare's audience (when the average was 40 for a man), and so perhaps there's something slightly fantastical in his experiences and stories:

OLD MAN
Three score and ten I remember well
Within the volume of which time I have seen
Hours dreadful and things strange; but this **sore** night
Hath **trifled** former knowings.

ROSS
                        Ha, good **Father**,
Thou seest the heavens, as troubled with man's act,
Threatens his bloody stage…

sore = *violent, harsh, dreadful*

trifled = *made meaningless*

Father = *not a biological or religious relationship, but a polite way of addressing an elderly man*

....

☞ **PLACES**   See the Map (p.22) for more locations named in the play

• *Colme-Kill / The sacred storehouse* – on the holy isle of Iona, where Scottish kings were buried
• *He is already named and gone to **Scone*** – the ancient royal city, where the Stone of Destiny lay, on which the new kings were crowned
• *I'll to **Fife*** – As Thane of Fife, this is Macduff's territory

Act 3:1

Location: *The Royal Palace, Forres*

Characters: *Banquo, Macbeth, Lady Macbeth, Lennox, Ross, Lords, Attendants, Servant, Two Murderers*

Action: *Banquo opens the scene talking about the Witches' prophecy, as if to Macbeth, before we see Macbeth and Lady Macbeth, successful in having gained the crown.*

....

☞ **CHARACTERS**   KING and QUEEN

The scene sees the first entrance of Macbeth and Lady as King and Queen; all the other characters should from hereon bow or kneel whenever they enter or leave a room. Macbeth seems very much in control as he plans his next move – even remembering the Witches' prophecy when he checks with Banquo about Fleance.

💬 SPEECH MACBETH

Note the gaps in the metre before Macbeth asks his 'casual' questions, trying to find out where Banquo will be, and the dramatic pause after Banquo's vows that he will not miss the feast – as indeed he does not:

MACBETH
To-night **we** hold a solemn supper, Sir,
And I'll request your presence.

BANQUO
                              Let your Highness
Command upon me, to the which my duties
Are with a most indissoluble tie
For ever knit. (x \ x \ x \ )

MACBETH
Ride you this afternoon?

BANQUO
                              Ay, my good lord.

MACBETH
We should have else desired your good advice,
(Which still hath been both **grave** and prosperous)
In this **day's council**; but we'll take to-morrow.
(x \ x \ x \ ) Is't far you ride?

BANQUO
As far, my lord, as will fill up the time
'Twixt this and supper: go not my horse the better,
I must become a borrower of the night,
For a dark hour, or **twain**.

MACBETH
                              Fail not our feast.

BANQUO
My lord, I will not. (x x \ x \ )

we – now King, Macbeth starts to use the royal 'we' instead of 'I' when speaking to others; although he uses 'I' in the next line – making the request extremely personal?

grave = serious

day's council – Macbeth is conducting the affairs of the State with his Thanes

twain = two

☞ CHARACTERS The MURDERERS

From what he says to them, it seems this isn't the first time Macbeth has spoken with the Murderers. Having apparently been very careful and persuasive beforehand, he's very direct in this scene. These men don't seem to be hardened or even competent professionals, as they're easily convinced that Banquo has persecuted them for years.

It's interesting that Macbeth dismisses Lady before conspiring with them; an element to Macbeth's character and the terrible things he's planning that no longer needs her support? Or perhaps he's trying to protect her, shield and keep her relatively innocent? Does he foresee her later confession-ridden breakdown?

☞ WORDS

• *an **unlineal** hand* = not of the same family, of different descent
• *mine **eternal jewel*** = my soul
• *the **common enemy of man*** = Satan, the Devil
• *leave **no rubs nor botches** in the work* = no inequality or mistakes; the murderers must kill Fleance too

Act 3:2

Location: *The Royal Palace, Forres*

Characters: *Lady Macbeth, Servant, Macbeth*

Action: *The first time we encounter Macbeth and Lady Macbeth alone together since the murder. Both have changed, considerably. Having made her husband King, she seems far less powerful despite now being Queen. While Macbeth takes the initiative, we witness his developing paranoia; but apparently both of them are having fearful dreams.*

☞ THOU/YOU

Notice that while Macbeth does still use *thou* to her, Lady only uses *you* to him. A continuation of the change in their relationship, which began in 1:7.

> ## 🗩 SPEECH LADY MACBETH
>
> Lady asks a Servant for some time with the King, an unusual turn to their marriage. She then immediately turns to us with a beautifully sad speech of two rhyming couplets, the first time she's spoken directly to us since her opening scene:
>
> **LADY**
> Say to the King I would attend his leisure   +1
> For a few words.
>
> **SERVANT**
>   Madam, I will.
>
> **LADY**
>   Naught's had, all's *spent*,   +1
> Where our desire is got without *content*:
> 'Tis safer to be that which we *destroy*,
> Than by destruction dwell in doubtful *joy*.
>
> She ends her next speech to Macbeth with *what's done is done* – a phrase that has since come into popular modern English use – note the finality and spare simplicity of the four sounds. Lady is being as pragmatic as she can:
>
> *Enter Macbeth*
>
> How now, <u>my lord?</u> Why do you keep alone,   +1
> Of sorriest fancies your companions making,
> Using those thoughts which should indeed have died
> With them <u>they think on?</u> Things without all
>   remedy   +2
> Should be without regard; what's <u>done is done.</u>
>
> **MACBETH**
> We have **scorch'd** the snake, not kill'd it; (x \ )   -2
> She'll close and be herself; whilst our poor malice   +1

scorch'd – slashed, as with a knife; the repeated K sound in this line makes him sound sharp and curt with her?

Remains in danger of <u>her former tooth.</u>
But let the frame of things disjoint, both the worlds
   suffer   +2
Ere we will eat our meal in fear, and sleep
In the affliction of these **terrible dreams**   +1
That <u>shake us nightly.</u> Better be with the dead +1
Whom we, to gain our peace, have sent to peace,
Than on the torture of the mind to lie
In <u>restless **ecstasy**.</u> Duncan is in his grave;   +1
After life's fitful fever he sleeps well;
Treason has done his worst; nor steel, nor poison,
Malice domestic, **foreign levy**, nothing   +1
Can <u>touch him further!</u>

terrible dreams – a
sudden eye into
Macbeth's life when
we haven't seen him:
'better to be dead
than toss and turn at
night with a tortured
mind'

ecstasy = madness

foreign levy = civil
war or demand from a
foreign country

☞ WORDS

- *make our faces* **vizards** *to our hearts* = mask, visor
- *be thou* **jocund** = merry, joyful, cheerful

Act 3:3

Location: *Near the Royal Palace, Forres*

Characters: *Three Murderers, Banquo, Fleance*

Action: *As the two Murderers wait to kill Banquo and Fleance – one of three on-stage murders in the play – a third Murderer unexpectedly joins them. It seems Macbeth doesn't trust anybody, not even the employees to whom he has given 'direction just' (exact instructions). The last scripted time we see Fleance.*

☞ CHARACTER THIRD MURDERER

Sometimes played by Macbeth in disguise. He's also been played as being a particularly clumsy or incompetent character, blamed for allowing Fleance to escape.

Act 3:4

Location: *Banquet hall, the Royal Palace, Forres*

Characters: *Macbeth, Lady Macbeth, Ross, Lennox, Lords, Attendants, First Murderer, Ghost of Banquo*

Action: *A very famous scene, often referred to as the Banquet Scene.*

A feast is being held by King Macbeth in honour of Banquo – although of course Macbeth knows his guest will not turn up. After the Murderer reports Banquo has been killed but that Fleance escaped, Macbeth toasts his comrade, and then sees his Ghost come to sit in Macbeth's seat. Lady Macbeth accuses her husband of hallucinating as he did the dagger, repeatedly challenging his manhood. By the end of the scene they both show signs of beginning to crumble.

....

☞ WORDS

• *you know **your own degrees*** = your own rank, station; they know the hierarchy of where they should sit in relation to him

• *thou art the **nonpareil*** = a person without equal, unique one, paragon

....

☞ CHARACTER BANQUO'S GHOST

Banquo enters shaking his head, pointing at Macbeth, silently accusing him of the murder, moving slowly, his hair and face covered in blood – *never shake / Thy gory locks at me* – a particularly famous line. The Ghost could equally be characterised by moving quickly, trying and failing to communicate to the others who his murderer is.

Productions compete for fresh effects here, with some having the Ghost appear from under the table, by masking his entrance with the other guests, or 'magically' appearing and disappearing in different parts of the stage.

💬 SPEECH MACBETH

There are gaps in the metre as Macbeth sees Banquo's Ghost, as Lennox is startled by his King's reaction, and as Ross makes the decision that they should leave:

MACBETH
Here had we now our country's honour roof'd,
Were the grac'd person of our Banquo present;

Enter the Ghost of Banquo, who sits in Macbeth's place

Who may I rather **challenge** for unkindness,
Than pity for mischance.

challenge ... mischance
= blame for rudeness
then pity for befalling
disaster

ROSS
               His absence, Sir,
Lays blame upon his promise. Please't your Highness
To grace us with your royal company?

MACBETH
The table's full.

LENNOX
             Here is a place reserv'd, Sir.

MACBETH
Where?

LENNOX
    Here, my good Lord.(x \ x \ x)
What is't that moves your Highness?(x \ x)

MACBETH
Which of you have done this?

LORDS
               What, my good Lord?

MACBETH
Thou canst not say, I did it; never shake
Thy gory locks at me. (x \ x \ )

ROSS
Gentlemen, rise; his Highness is not well.

⤷ WORDS

• *our monuments / Shall be the **maws of kites*** = mouths of birds of prey

• *the **Hyrcan Tiger*** = a tiger of Hyrcania, a province of Persia, now Iran; proverbial for its ferocity

---

○ SPEECH MACBETH

Macbeth talks of birds (as Lady Macduff does later in 4:2) and superstitions, then decides to visit the Weird Sisters again. The birds that are mentioned all eat carrion (including corpses) and can all be taught to speak – a popular folklore held in Shakespeare's time said that these birds could denounce crime and criminals (men of blood):

MACBETH
It will have blood, they say: blood will have blood:
Stones have been known to move, and trees to speak;
Augures, and understood relations, have
By **magot-pies**, and **choughs**, and rooks, brought forth
The secret'st man of blood.

augures = prophecy, divination

magot-pies = magpies

choughs = jackdaws

Act 3:5

Location: *A Heath near Forres*

Characters: *Three Witches, Hecate*

Action: *Hecate berates the Witches for telling Macbeth his future without her help. This is one of the two collaboratively written scenes; often cut from a production.*

....

⤷ CHARACTER HECATE

The Greek goddess of the Underworld, associated with magic, ghosts and witches, and very powerful. Many doubt that Shakespeare wrote these lines (see AFTER pp.84–5), but the addition makes it interesting to see that the Witches are subservient to another, and are not supreme in their power. Note that Hecate also speaks in iambic tetrameter, as the Witches often do.

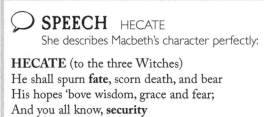

💬 **SPEECH** HECATE

She describes Macbeth's character perfectly:

HECATE (to the three Witches)
He shall spurn **fate**, scorn death, and bear   **fate** = destiny
His hopes 'bove wisdom, grace and fear;
And you all know, **security**   **security** = over-
Is mortals' chiefest enemy.   confidence, not safety

🔖 **WORDS**

- **beldams** as you are = hags
- at the pit of **Acheron** / Meet me i'th'morning = in classical mythology, the chasm or abyss of the Underworld; also the name of one of the rivers there, traditionally black, past which the souls of the dead have to cross after death

Act 3:6

Location: The Royal Palace, Forres

Characters: Lennox, Lord

Action: Lennox meets a Lord, who tells of Malcolm's flight to England and his joining forces with Northumberland's English powers. He reports Macduff's rebelling against Macbeth (who is described as a 'hand accurs'd') and reflects on the suffering of Scotland.

The scene is an important turning point in the play, offering a hint of optimism in the face of the fall of Scotland under Macbeth's tyranny.

⊃ SPEECH LORD

The nameless Lord has a packed little speech, referring to six different characters, using alternate names for many of them:

LORD

                         The **son** of Duncan
From whom this **tyrant** holds the **due of birth**,
Lives in the English Court, and is received
Of the most **pious Edward** with such grace,
That the **malevolence** of Fortune nothing
Takes from <u>his high respect.</u> Thither Macduff
Is gone to pray the Holy King, upon his aid
To **wake Northumberland**, <u>and warlike **Siward**.</u>

son *of Duncan =* Malcolm

tyrant *= Macbeth*

due of birth *– his inheritance of the throne by birthright*

pious *= religious, holy*

Edward *– the Confessor, King of England (1042–1066)*

the malevolence ... respect *– Malcolm is still held in high regard despite suffering ill-fortune*

wake *= persuade to act*

Northumberland *– Earl of Northumberland and English general allied to Malcolm*

Siward *– Northumberland's 'warlike' son, later referred to as Young Siward*

Act 4:1

Location: *A cavern near Forres. In the middle, a boiling cauldron*

Characters: *Three Witches, Hecate, Macbeth, First Apparition, Second Apparition, Third Apparition, Apparitions of Kings, Apparition of Banquo, Lennox*

Action: *Macbeth returns to the Witches. Now King, he wants to ensure he remains so. After hearing new prophecies, Lennox arrives with the news of Macduff's reported escape to England, and Macbeth plans revenge on Macduff's family.*

Set around a cauldron, it can be a vivid scene, allowing great scope in terms of design options.

The 'Double, double…' chant of the Witches brings an echo of their opening scene, and no other scene in Shakespeare brings together so many ominous words and phrases connected with the black arts.

....

☞ SIDE-NOTE The APPARITIONS

The Witches show Macbeth three apparitions:

> **an armed* head**, tells him to beware of Macduff, the Thane of Fife
>
> **a bloody child**, tells him he needs to fear 'no man born of woman'
>
> **a crowned child with a tree in its hand**, tells him that Macbeth will remain King until the wood in Birnam comes to Dunsinane Hill

*armed head – the meaning of this is disputed; a head wearing a helmet? Macbeth's own severed head, a forecast of what is to come?

Macbeth dismisses the second and third apparitions, as, of course, every man is born from a woman, and a wood cannot walk to a castle.

As we'll see, there is huge irony in his pleased response (*Sweet bodements* = wonderful omens) to these prophecies. But his pleasure is halted when he asks about a descendant of Banquo becoming king – and he is shown a family-line of eight kings, the last looking very much like Banquo.

....

☞ WORDS

- *Harpier cries* = the third Witch's familiar: *an owl*, or *a harpy* = a mythical bird, half woman, half vulture
- *a tiger's* **chaudron** = the tiger's entrails
- *secret, **black** and midnight hags* = those who practise dark, or black, magic
- *her nine **farrow*** = litter; her nine piglets

Act 4:2

Location: *Macduff's castle, Fife*

Characters: *Lady Macduff, Son, Ross, Messenger, Murderers*

Action: *This scene features one of the most brutal and horrifically cold-blooded murders in the entire Shakespeare canon, comparable to Gloucester's eyes being put out in 3:7 of King Lear.*

The murders are savage, unstylised, and the rough, straight-forward attitude of the Murderers make them seem somehow like they aren't in a play at all; that this is a horrifically matter-of-fact depiction of how real people become victims of oppression in civil war.

Lady Macduff struggles to understand why her husband has fled to England without explanation, and she tells her son his father is dead, and a traitor. Murderers, paid by Macbeth, arrive soon after she is warned by a Messenger to flee.

The mother-son exchange is an odd one – her peremptory tone and his directness brings a jocular quality to a scene book-ended in darkness.

Is Lady Macduff trying to keep her son's spirits up? Or perhaps Shakespeare is setting his audience up for a fall with a moment of comedy before the coming tragedy.

A great part of the horror of the scene is that Shakespeare hasn't described exactly how Lady Macduff is murdered, leaving exactly what they do to her either off-stage in the audience's imaginations, or on-stage and filled with the director's imagination.

💬 SPEECH LADY MACDUFF

Lady Macduff's bird analogies to her son are reiterated with Macduff's *All my pretty chickens* in the next scene:

LADY MACDUFF
Poor bird, thou'dst never fear the net, nor **lime**, the **pitfall** nor the **gin**!

lime = the birdlime (used to catch birds)
pitfall = the birdtrap
gin = the snare/trap

Act 4:3

Location: *The Court of the English King, England*

Characters: *Malcolm, Macduff, Doctor, Ross*

Action: *Generally regarded as a difficult scene to act to and sit through. It's the longest scene in the play, and opens with a relatively lengthy (114 line) dialogue, just as the play is really starting to pick up pace again.*

Macbeth is now referred to as a 'tyrant', and we know he has had Macduff's family brutally murdered. Macduff has unwittingly escaped the same murderers by coming to the English court to seek out Prince Malcolm, who has been in hiding since his father's murder.

Macduff wants Malcolm to join forces and lead an army against Macbeth. But Macbeth has already tried to win Malcolm over by sending him supposed friends, so the young Prince tests Macduff's loyalty by pretending to be a supporter of Macbeth's tyranny, before finally revealing his true allegiance.

*A brief passage with a Doctor tells of the good King Edward's healing of a sickness ('tis called the **Evil** = scrofula), and the tales of Edward's pious nature contrast heavily with those of Macbeth's tyranny. The scene also brilliantly mirrors the*

*situation in Scotland: here in England, we hear of a good king
who is healing his loyal subjects, while in Scotland there is a*
poor Country, / Almost afraid to know itself.

*Acted well, the first half of this scene can be a fascinating
game of cat and mouse, while the latter half sees Macduff
receive the news of his family, and can be utterly, devastatingly
heart-breaking.*

☞ THOU / YOU

As Malcolm tests Macduff's loyalty, he sticks to the formal
you throughout. Macduff switches back and forth, from his
contemptuous *Fare* **thee** *well Lord* to his attempt at support
a few moments later with *fear not yet / To take upon* **you**
what is yours.

Malcolm switches back to using *thee* when he comes clean
with Macduff, although his speech of admission ends with a
peculiar switch back to a more formal *Why are* **you** *silent?*,
perhaps as the bemused Macduff struggles to take all the
new information in:

MALCOLM
What I am truly,

Is **thine,** and my poor country's, to command:
Whither, indeed, before **thy** here-approach,
Old Siward, with ten thousand warlike men,
Already at a point, <u>was setting forth.</u>
Now we'll together; and the chance of goodness
Be like our <u>warranted quarrel.</u> Why <u>are **you** silent?</u>   +2

MACDUFF
Such welcome, and unwelcome things at once
'Tis hard to reconcile.

☞ WORDS

• *the title is* **affer'd** = Macbeth's status as tyrant has been
legally confirmed
• *I grant him bloody,* **luxurious... sudden** = lusftful... violent;
the full range of Macbeth's vices is now laid bare
• *wiped the black* **scruples** = suspicions

- *never was **forsworn*** = to break your word
- *ten thousand warlike men/Already **at a point*** = ready for war; Malcolm has already called on Siward for reinforcements
- *a **fee-grief**, / Due to some single breast* = a grief with just one owner; Macduff already senses the news is bad

---

💬 SPEECH ROSS

A gap in the metre, presumably as Ross hesitates before briefly equivocating to Macduff about the health of his children:

> **MACDUFF**
> How does my wife?

> **ROSS**
> 1–2   Why, well.

> **MACDUFF**
> 3–7   And all my children?

> **ROSS**
> 9–10   (x) Well too.

Act 5:1

Location: *Macbeth's castle, Dunsinane*

Characters: *Doctor of Physic, Waiting-Gentlewoman, Lady Macbeth*

Action: *Sometimes referred to as the Sleep-walking Scene.*

The first time we see Lady Macbeth since the Banquet Scene. We hear she has been repeatedly sleep-walking and sleep-talking, while rubbing her hands. Concerned for her well-being, the woman attending on her has brought a doctor. Both the Gentlewoman and the Doctor equivocate – neither can bear to say they now know the truth about Duncan's murder.

It's a stark scene evoking many strong images, and has given us some memorable lines: Out, damned spot! *and* Hell is murky, *as well as beautifully poetic ones* All the perfumes of Arabia will not sweeten this little hand.

....

☞ SIDE-NOTE   *'to seem thus washing her hands'*

Witches were believed to have renounced their baptism by water, so in theory water cannot touch a witch. For Shakespeare's audience, Lady Macbeth has become very witch-like.

The Doctor sees in Lady Macbeth's behaviour *a great pertur-bation in nature* (a disturbance in her mental health): getting the benefits of sleep while at the same time acting as if being awake: another image of the world turned upside-down by the murder of Duncan. See AFTER (pp.81–3) for more on insomnia.

○ SPEECH   DOCTOR

In some productions, a moment of humour can be played with the Doctor's question, balancing well the tragedy of Lady's sleep-walking:

LADY	To bed, to bed, to bed. [Exits]
DOCTOR	(to Waiting-Gentlewoman) Will she go now to bed?
GENT.	Directly.

....

☞ WORDS

- *none can call our power to* **accompt** = reckoning, judgment [especially by God]
- *with this* **starting** = startled reaction, flinching, recoiling
- *my mind she has* **mated** = bewildered, confounded

66

Act 5:2

Location: *Countryside near Macbeth's castle, Dunsinane*

Characters: *Menteth, Cathness, Angus, Lennox, Soldiers*

Action: *From hereon, the scenes are shorter and the play picks up pace again as the English powers led by Malcolm, Macduff and Siward advance towards Dunsinane, where Macbeth waits and prepares for war.*

A straight forward scene. With the first show of Scottish rebel power, four of Macbeth's Thanes discuss where they will meet the English powers. They are rebelling against Macbeth, who – despite being tyrannical – is still their king; perhaps there is a sense that they are reluctant to take arms against him?

....

🖙 WORDS

- *the English **power** is near* = armed force, troops, host, army
- *his **distempered** cause* = insane, deranged, lunatic
- *the sickly **weal*** = state, community, commonwealth

Act 5:3

Location: *Macbeth's castle, Dunsinane*

Characters: *Macbeth, Doctor, Attendants, Servant, Seyton*

Action: *Thinking himself secure and invincible with the knowledge the Witches gave him, Macbeth shrugs off news of the advancing English army, and taunts the Doctor to cure Lady's mind-sickness.*

We see the warrior perhaps at his most tyrannical and tragic moment, blindly ordering what few followers he has left, and ignoring all advice they give. Macbeth's verse is very broken in this scene; as he rejects the Doctor's advice about his wife, he is nothing less than terrifying.

💬 SPEECH MACBETH

At the same time as Macbeth rants, he is also given lines of great poetry. He realises what he has lost, and what he will never have in life, making it hard not to sympathise for him:

MACBETH

I have liv'd long enough: my way of life
Is **fall'n into the sere**, the yellow leaf;
And that which should accompany old age,
As honour, love, obedience, troops of friends,
I must not look to have; but in their stead
Curses, not loud, but deep, **mouth-honour**, breath,
Which the poor heart would fain deny, <u>and dare not</u>.

*fall'n into the sere =
dried up, withered,
parched*

*mouth-honour –
honour shown in word
not deed*

🖙 WORDS

- *Where gott'st thou that **goose** look?* = stupid, foolish, idiotic
- ***cast** the water of the land* = examine the urine of every person in the country to find a cause for Lady Macbeth's sickness; the line compares Scotland to a diseased patient
- ***purge** it to a sound and pristine health* = remove it; sickness was thought of something that could be removed
- *I would applaud thee to the very **Echo*** = I would applaud so hard the God of Echo would applaud back
- *What rhubarb, **senna***, or what purgative drug* = a variety of shrub which produces a drug causing vomiting and bowel evacuation;

*in some editions of the text, printed as **cyme** = the head of a plant and another drug which induces vomiting

Act 5:4

Location: *Countryside near Birnam wood, 15 miles from Macbeth's Castle at Dunsinane*

Characters: *Malcolm, Siward, Macduff, Young Siward, Menteth, Cathness, Angus, Lennox, Ross, Soldiers*

Action: *The rebels massed, Malcolm hits on the idea of disguising their numbers with branches from the nearby wood. The first of the Witches' warnings – and Shakespeare's tricks – comes true: Birnam Wood comes to Dunsinane.*

Note that all the Thanes from the earlier part of the play have now changed sides, and are fighting to bring Macbeth's reign to an end.

....

☞ TEXT   EDITION VARIATIONS

Depending on which text has been used, the remaining scenes are broken up differently. Some editions of the play do not make scene changes here, but keep the action going in one continuous scene through to the end.

....

☞ WORDS

* *both **more and less** have given him the revolt* = men of high and low rank have rebelled
* *none serve with him but **constrained** things/Whose hearts are absent too* = forced (all those fighting with Macbeth are unwilling)

Act 5:5

Location: *Macbeth's castle, Dunsinane*

Characters: *Macbeth, Seyton, Soldiers, Messenger*

Action: *As Macbeth prepares for battle, news of his wife's death brings a tragic island of calm to his whirlwind-like mind. It results in one of the most famous speeches in the play, and we hear a reflective element from Macbeth that we have not heard before.*

💬 SPEECH MACBETH

The reaction to the news of his wife's death. 12 lines; 4 thoughts, 2 mid-line, 1 metrically short; 1 exclamation.

The metrically short line *She should have died hereafter* has been interpreted to mean 'she would have died anyway', 'she would have been killed along with me later', 'death is inevitable' and that he doesn't care, and plenty more. Whatever choice is made, the news appears to be the last straw for Macbeth.

Tomorrow, and tomorrow, and tomorrow could be the eternal days of the *hereafter*; some future time that never comes when Lady could have died; Macbeth's own exhaustion at life's relentless barrage; or perhaps something else?

It's one of the most famous speeches in the play, and every line in it has become well-known. The verse is slightly more regular than the frenzied speech earlier in the scene, and the news of Lady's death seems to oddly quieten Macbeth:

Enter Seyton

MACBETH
                Wherefore was that cry?

SEYTON
The queen, my lord, is dead. (x \ x \)   **-4**

MACBETH
She should have <u>died hereafter.</u> (\ x \)   **-3**
There would have been a time for such a word –
To-morrow, and to-morrow, and to-morrow,   **+1**
Creeps in this petty pace from day to day
To the last syllable of recorded time;
And all our yesterdays have lighted fools
The way <u>to dusty death.</u> Out, out, **brief candle!**   **+1**
Life's but a walking shadow, a poor **player**   **+1**
That struts and frets his hour upon the stage
And then is heard no more: it is a tale
Told by an idiot, full of sound and fury,   **+1**
<u>Signifying nothing.</u>

x \ – two gaps in the metre – as Macbeth takes in the news of his wife's death?

brief candle – a reference to Lady Macbeth's life (hers is the last candle we saw)? A candle he's holding?

player = actor

In 'tomorrow, and tomorrow, and tomorrow', the important word is 'and'…

Sir Ian McKellen to Sir Patrick Stewart, 2008

💬 SPEECH   MACBETH

The combination of Lady Macbeth's death and the news that he has been duped by the Witches' prophecy begins to pull Macbeth down. His courage remains, though – a redeeming feature, even in one so tyrannical:

MACBETH
I 'gin to be **aweary of the sun,**
And wish th' estate o'th world were now undone –
Ring the <u>alarum bell!</u> – **Blow wind,** come wrack!
At least we'll die with **harness** <u>on our back.</u>
Exeunt

aweary of the sun – if the tragedy of Macbeth's life had not been clear before, this sound of defeat is crushing

Blow wind – see King Lear – 'Blow, winds and crack thy cheeks' – calling on Nature to help

harness = armour

☞ WORDS

• *Till famine and the **ague** eat them up* = fever, sickness, shaking (the kind caused by a fever)

- Were they not **forc'd** with those that should be ours = reinforced; in some editions of the text the word is **farced** = stuffed, crammed
- If they speech be **sooth** = true; thus the term *Soothsayer*, found in other plays
- begin / To doubt the equivocation of the fiend/That lies **like truth** = begin to realise how the Witches lied

Act 5:6

Location: *Outside Macbeth's castle, Dunsinane*

Characters: *Malcolm, Siward, Macduff*

Action: *Another short straight-forward scene. The beginning of the war between Macbeth's forces and those of Malcolm. Note that hereon, Malcolm refers to himself using the royal 'we'.*

💬 **SPEECH** MALCOLM
Leading the English forces, who, having covered themselves with the boughs of Birnam Wood, have successfully reached Macbeth's castle. He orders his generals:

MALCOLM
Now, near enough, your leafy screens throw down
And show like those you are. You, **worthy uncle,**
Shall with my **cousin** your right noble son,
Lead our first battle.

worthy uncle =
Siward, the Earl of Northumberland
cousin = *Young Siward*

··

☞ **WORDS**

- *harbingers* of blood and death = forerunners

Act 5:7

Location: *Outside Macbeth's castle, Dunsinane*

Characters: *Macbeth, Young Siward, Macduff, Malcolm, Siward*

Action: *Now in battle, Macbeth brags that none of woman born can kill him. He fights with Young Siward and kills him (we find out in the last scene from Ross he was killed by a sword thrust through his chest), though we quickly hear that Macbeth's castle has surrendered.*

☞ WORDS

- *the castle's gently **rendered*** = tamely surrendered
- *I cannot strike at wretched **Kernes*** = mercenaries; Macduff's fight is not with hired men
- *one of greatest note / Seems **bruited*** = reported; he hears Macbeth fighting near-by

Act 5:8

Location: *Outside Macbeth's castle, Dunsinane*

Characters: *Macbeth, Macduff*

Action: *Macbeth and Macduff finally meet in battle, and the true nature of Macduff's birth and the Witches' prophecies are revealed. Macduff was born by Caesarean section – untimely ripped – a crucial and famous phrase.*

💬 SPEECH MACBETH

We discover the full extent of the Witches' equivocation, and the final part of Macbeth's downfall:

MACBETH
I bear a charmed life, which must not yield
To one of woman born.

MACDUFF
                              Despair thy charm;
And let the **Angel** whom thou still hast serv'd
Tell thee, Macduff was from his mother's womb
Untimely ripp'd.   (x \ x \ x \ )

MACBETH
Accursed be that tongue that tells me so;
For it has **cow'd** my better part of man

*the **Angel** = the bad spirit, or demon*

x \ – as Macbeth realises his error in believing the Witches' prophecy so wholly

***cow'd** – intimidated*

....

👉 WORDS

- *intrenchant* air = uncuttable, incapable of being gashed
- *these juggling* fiends = deceiving, cheating
- *that palter* with us = deal evasively

Act 5:9

Location: *Macbeth's castle, Dunsinane*

Characters: *Malcolm, Siward, Ross, Thanes, Soldiers, Macduff*

Action: *Siward receives news of his son's death, Macduff brings on Macbeth's head, having just decapitated it, and Malcolm is proclaimed King.*

⬭ SPEECH   MACDUFF

Macduff has cut off Macbeth's head, and carries it on-stage, presumably by the hair. Modern productions often have him carry a bloodied sack, to avoid the complications (and possible laughter) that can be triggered by an ill-made fake decapitated head:

MACDUFF
Hail, <u>King!</u> For <u>so thou art.</u> Behold where stands
The usurper's cursed head: **the time is free.**
I see thee **compassed** with thy kingdom's pearl

the time is free
– Shakespeare sometimes writes four simple words and the multitude of meanings is astonishing; essentially, 'Liberty has been restored'

compassed –
surrounded; Macduff envisages Malcolm crowned as King

⬭ SPEECH   MALCOLM

Malcolm's final speech closes the play, rewarding all with earldoms, and starts a new era in Scottish history. The speech has several words of hope: *loves*, *friends*, *grace* and *thanks*. The speech – and the play – ends with a rhyming couplet that unfortunately, in most English modern accents, no longer rhymes:

MALCOLM
So thanks to all at once, and to each **one,**
Whom we invite to see us crowned at **Scone.**

....

☞ WORDS

• *some must* **go off** = die, pass away
• *Had he his hurts* **before**? = was he wounded in the front?
• *paid his* **score** = reckoning, account (he died free of his sins)
• *by* **self and violent hands** / *Took off her life* = by her own violent hands (she committed suicide)

AFTER

It's been bugging me. It's got under my skin. I think it's a play completely different from his other work. It's about a life going into stasis. And that's a very difficult thing to do theatrically.

Simon Russell-Beale, 2013

I like this play, but it's the one I had to work hardest at – thanks to memories of confusing studies at school. Now, it's one of the most fascinating parts of the canon to me.

It comes about 15 years into Shakespeare's theatrical career (most of it spent with the same group of actors) and there's something muscular and lean about the way he uses the metre throughout which I deeply admire.

The staggered, stairway-like effect in the exchange in 2:2 (p.45, when Macbeth returns to his wife having murdered Duncan), is the extract I always use to explain how Shakespeare can orchestrate the dramatic pacing of a scene from four centuries away.

By this point in the canon he was ably using the metre to help show his actors when they should pause, and when they shouldn't – writing fast, snappy dialogue instead of long set piece speeches, but dialogue that also happened to be poetic. Despite that solid metrical framework underpinning everything, rather than restricting character interpretation, it blows options wide open with unanswered questions.

It's a play that is a re-run in some respects of his earlier *Richard III* and *Julius Caesar*, featuring a slow build-up towards murdering the rightful leader in the first half, with the second half concentrating on the emotional and psychological fallout of such actions – much like the structure of Alfred Hitchcock's film *Psycho*.

CANON

When Shakespeare wrote *Macbeth* he had just written *Timon of Athens* and the group of plays that came to be called the 'problem' plays – problematic because they were neither comedy nor tragedy. Having explored mixing the two genres so perfectly in *Twelfth Night*, there are much darker hearts beating at the cores of the comedic *All's Well That Ends Well* and *Measure for Measure*.

Othello, King Lear, Macbeth, Antony and Cleopatra, Pericles, Coriolanus and *The Winter's Tale* followed – huge, titanic works, each exploring the fall of a good man, but from a slightly different angle each time.

Othello suffers at the hands of another, Lear is foolish, and Leontes (in *The Winter's Tale*) is susceptible to jealousy, as we all are, but Macbeth becomes a tyrant, a killer of innocents, like Richard III – although perhaps without Richard's charm, as he rashly strikes out in every direction.

This makes Macbeth hard to sympathise with by the end. The last shred of sympathy for him is often used up when Lady Macbeth dies. From thereon he feels like a man with nothing left to lose, although a form of pity for his tragic end is often reignited if the actor lets us see a look of shock during his final encounter with Macduff, as all the pieces of the puzzle fall into place for him.

When you see someone run around like that in a piece of theatre, especially if they rely on a coven of Witches for advice, you know it's only a matter of time before they're done for. And yet he still makes for a great dramatic figure, someone who is aware they're trapped in a downward spiral and decides to plunge headlong down anyway.

THEMATIC

Shakespeare's works are often discussed thematically, and themes are important because they draw attention to parallels between then and now. But they're not the whole story. Four centuries on, we can identify with ambition, jealousy, self-doubt, and so on, but it's characters that make themes, not themes that make characters. Underneath the speeches are characters that think and feel like any other living person. And that's the starting point.

Whatever *Macbeth* is, Shakespeare didn't set out to write a play about a particular theme. Macbeth doesn't reach for the crown to explore the theme of ambition. He is ambitious, and so it's easy to read that theme into the play. Lady Macbeth is a strong woman, so it's a play about feminism too.

It can equally be a play about the current conflicts around the world, democracy, or any number of things – depending on the depth of reading you give the text. The caesarian section that brings Macduff into the world would very likely have killed his mother, and indeed the play is underpinned by the themes of motherhood, infanticide and childbirth, too.

A marvellous thing about Shakespeare's plays is that we can use them to reflect or refract virtually any modern political or sociological theme, freely channelling ideologies through his writing as if he wrote them to be sponges sucking up whatever part of life we bring to them.

THE MACBETHS

If Aragorn in *The Lord of the Rings* had taken the Ring and Arwen had turned to Mordor, he would have become Macbeth, and she, Lady Macbeth, essentially, takes the Ring. He's Al Pacino's Jonny in *Scarface*, too. I've recommended the film in the list below (p.94). It's certified for viewers over the age of 18, but there are far worse horrors in this often school-studied play.

Is he the intelligent man in his 20s or early 30s fighting for the throne – a shade of Hamlet? Or is he more like Coriolanus, the loyal fighting machine unused to public speaking and sacrificing himself for his beliefs? Or then again, is he a young, reckless Romeo figure, mixed with hints of the clever and manipulative killer-king Richard III? Whatever his actual years, he has not yet gained the wisdom that usually comes with age to see past the Witches' equivocation. Impulsively trusting at first, Macbeth believes the Witches are is terrified by Banquo's Ghost. He then becomes paranoid to the point of excluding everyone from his side, apart from a character called Seyton.

Lady Macbeth is different – we watch as she embraces her own darkness, and then see her left far behind having encouraged her husband to engage with his own inner demons. She loses her mind in a waking-dream, hallucinating blood on her hands, and possibly ends her own life (it's not specified how she dies). So equally, Lady could be 60 or 20; an older life-partner or a new wife. Interestingly, productions have been casting younger and younger actresses in the part in recent years.

The baby she talks about in 1:7 – *I have given suck, and know / How tender 'tis to love the babe that milks me* – might have been from a previous marriage that Macbeth wasn't a part of, meaning their relationship is relatively new, or they might have been together for many years, and the lost baby is theirs.

This is a famous open question in the play, and the production can spin towards or away from it – Macduff's line *He has no children* in 4:3 could refer to Macbeth, or it could be a criticism of the slightly inept way Ross delivered the news to Macduff.

The casting of the lead characters of any production is hugely important, whether it's Romeo and Juliet, or Beatrice and Benedict (in *Much Ado About Nothing*), and if the audience doesn't buy into these relationships, then the production is in trouble.

This is a tragedy driven forward not by a solitary figure but a married couple, reminiscent of Cornwall and Regan's subplot in *King Lear*. Part of the joy of watching different productions of *Macbeth* is seeing how the actors portray the disintegration of this relationship in particular – they only have a few scenes together, so we need to quickly believe they are a couple in a strong relationship; that they could plot and carry out a murder together. Some productions make the Macbeths an overtly sexual couple, others try to suggest that their strength – or ensuing disintegration – comes from having lost that baby.

The characters are based on real historical figures, but there's a point where you decide when to follow the true history of events, and when to part from them, to tell a particular type of story. And every decision made will completely alter an audience's experience of the play.

MACBETH DOES MURDER SLEEP

I like Macbeth. He's a weird animal. The character of a warrior with a very poetic heart. The verse Shakespeare wrote for him is muscular, erratic, and the imagery is incredibly powerful. From the terrifying:

O full of scorpions is my mind, dear wife.

To the child-like rhyming:

> *I will not be afraid of Death and* Bane
> *Till Birnam Wood come to* Dunsinane.

To the near-suicidal:

> *I 'gin to be a-weary of the Sun*
> *And wish th'estate o'th world were now undone.*

To elegiac reflection:

> *Tomorrow, and tomorrow, and tomorrow*
> *Creeps in this petty pace from day to day*
> *To the last syllable of recorded time.*

For me, one of the most hauntingly tragic moments is when, having murdered Duncan, Macbeth tells his wife:

> *Methought, I heard a voice cry, 'Sleep no more!*
> *Macbeth does murder Sleep'...*

He's describing the medical condition of *insomnia* – a term that isn't recorded in English until 1623, when it was defined in this way:

> *Insomnie* – watching; want of power to sleepe

Indeed, 'watching' is listed in the Bills of Mortality – a weekly list in Shakespeare's time, of who died of what. Essentially, *watching* is an inability to sleep; and Macbeth tell us the sleep that does come only brings nightmares

>   *and sleep*
> *In the affliction of these terrible dreams,*
> *That shake us nightly. Better be with the dead,*
> *Whom we, to gain our peace, have sent to peace,*
> *Than on the torture of the mind to lie*
> *In restless ecstasy.*

We know now that a human deprived of sleep for too long will slowly be driven mad, and can die. As the Doctor brought in by Lady Macbeth's Gentlewoman says

> *This disease is beyond my practice; yet I have known those which have walked in their sleep who have died holily in their beds.*

The modern word *insomnia* didn't appear in the English language until 1758, seven years before the first victim of Fatal Insomnia was recorded in Venice, Italy. Oddly enough, bearing in mind what happens to Macbeth and Lady, the four stages of Fatal Insomnia are now known to be:

1 – up to 4 months of sleeplessness: brings on panic attacks, phobias and paranoia

Macbeth begins to experience fits during the play. In the Banquet Scene (3:4), it's worth noting Macbeth's *Then comes my fit again*, and Lady Macbeth, too:

> *My Lord is often thus,*
> *And hath been from his youth: pray you, keep seat;*
> *The fit is momentary.*

Later, at the end of the scene, Lady says to her husband *You lack the season of all natures, sleep* so both references to *fits* could be the panic attacks symptomatic of insomnia.

2 – over the next 5 months: hallucinations occur

A modern word for what both Macbeth (with the *air-drawn dagger*) and Lady Macbeth (seeing blood on her hands) go through.

3 – over the next 3 months: a complete inability to sleep will be followed by rapid weight loss

Which is obviously not an easy thing to stage in the theatre, but would be easier to show in a film version of the play.

4 – over the next 6 months: dementia, a lack of physical or verbal response to others

Which could be an interesting choice for Macbeth's metrical gaps later in the play, and allow for silent appearances of Lady Macbeth to be inserted before her Sleep-walking Scene (5:1).

Other symptoms of long-term sleep loss are menopause in women and impotence in men. Both are fascinating possible character choices, especially considering Lady Macbeth's reference to losing a child. Equally so, as she lambasts Macbeth's manliness, prompting his *I dare do all that may become a man*, and, after seeing Banquo's Ghost, his *I am a man again*.

THE WITCHES, THE CURSE, AND A BLOODY MARY

Everything has its opposite. Fair and foul. And, of course, there are two sides to the Witches' equivocation. They're some of the most extraordinary characters Shakespeare wrote. In writing them he tapped into his audience's greatest fear and gave the English theatre three characters with the most open frame.

There's nothing in this twenty-first-century world that terrifies us and makes us as paranoid on a daily basis as witches would have been to Shakespeare's audience. If Shakespeare's greatest parts are blank canvases, built on the most ornate and beautiful frames of metre, then anyone can play Hamlet, and paint their own image of him. But the Witches in *Macbeth* can be absolutely *anything*.

Their language is sparse, the imagery seems brittle like sun-bleached bone.

They are the stuff of nightmares, and are your worst nightmare. They're old crones, or young children. Puppets or voices and shifts of light. Blind, or psychic – or both. And they've been played in all these ways in productions over the last few decades.

But for me they have to be *scary*. Some designers and actors relish the opportunity for such creative freedom, while others dread the parts – looking or being scary isn't easy, if you think about it – and the quality of *scariness* dissipates immediately when there's the slightest sense of awkwardness or embarrassment about Being A Witch.

As it happens, although they are called *witches* in the stage directions, these characters are only referred to as *witches* in the text of the play once – the First Witch tells how she asked a Sailor's Wife for a chestnut, and the Wife replied

Aroynt thee, witch... (Get away, witch)

They call themselves (or are referred to) as the *weird* or *weyward sisters,* and indeed *weird* would have been pronounced more like *wayrd*, in those days. To Shakespeare's audience, the word *Witch* meant *enchanter, magician,* or *wizard* – all slightly magical and ethereal names to us.

Thanks to the idea of The Curse, even now, the play carries a peculiar negative energy with it. The very idea of the curse can feel as tangible as the shoes you wear, and some people will get very upset if the play is named outside of rehearsal or performance. The name continues to put a mystery in the air. Superstition keeps a bad smell hanging around in a rehearsal room if the name is said, even if no one present really believes anything will happen (but then, *it might...*)

It comes from the notion that demons and spirits were believed to be commandable if you could speak their name – an idea Shakespeare used with Oberon, who knows Puck's real name in *A Midsummer Night's Dream*, and Prospero, who knows Ariel's in *The Tempest*. America has a similar lore – the ghost-witch Bloody Mary, who will appear if you say her name.

HECATE, MIDDLETON, SHAKESPEARE

There's an idea that everything under Shakespeare's name was written by Shakespeare, and it's simply not true. A few of his later plays and a couple of his earlier ones were collaborations. The texts have been scrutinised by computer or compared to other texts of the time, and those who know, know.

Collaboration was a common practice in the theatres then, and young writers wrote to their strengths, whether they excelled in plot, character, verse or prose. Some say that the lines spoken by Hecate in 3:5 were written by one of Shakespeare's collaborators, Thomas Middleton, who is thought to have added the lines long after the play was first performed. Most are convinced of his participation because the song 'Come away, come away' (mentioned in stage direction and sung by the Witches to send off Hecate) is found in a later Middleton play called *The Witch*.

Hecate's lines are criticised as being coarse and colloquial – as a result, the scene is often cut from modern productions. Others argue that she speaks in rhyme and the same odd four-beat rhythm (iambic tetrameter) as the Witches, and so the lines are *supposed* to be unsettlingly different to the bulk of the rest of the play... It's a question that will probably remain open forever.

THE VISIONS – THE DAGGER, THE GHOST, THE AGE OF KINGS

THE DAGGER

In Shakespeare's time the dagger would, very likely, have been imaginary. Turning the metaphorical into the physical was something Shakespeare's audience were interested in – or rather, the opposite. The alchemists wanted to turn metal into gold and the philosophers wondered if the act of thought could create real objects.

With modern special effects the options for interpreting the moment have become much wider. Recent productions have had the Witches 'invisibly' hold the dagger in front of Macbeth, and then hand it to him as he reaches for it. It has been a mirrored illusion, or (in *uMabatha*, the 1970 play by Welcome Msomi), a hallucination brought on by a little sniff of something to calm Macbeth's nerves and give him the courage he needs.

But despite these recent reinventions, it's worth bearing in mind that Shakespeare's audience were more used to story-telling without special effects than we are, and that their imaginations were a powerful enough source for creation, without a need for visual crutches. The words were enough.

BANQUO'S GHOST

Ghosts often appear in Shakespeare's plays when the King's true successor hasn't taken over – modern Rock 'n' Roll fans would say this is why Elvis Presley keeps 'appearing'. Banquo's Ghost appears because Macbeth has unrightfully taken the crown, an unspoken theme that Shakespeare's audience would immediately have noticed.

A great part of his audience believed that ghosts existed. It was less common for people to think such an apparition was a hallucination of some kind, or a trick of the light. Our modern image of a ghost as a white sheet with eyes and a mouth cut in comes from their time, when the corpses of poor people were covered in white lime powder, before being wrapped in sheets. But for Shakespeare's audience, ghosts were imagined to be reanimated corpses, as substantial as zombies.

Covered in blood and pale-faced is less scary to an audience desensitised by Hollywood movies, so lighting and sound effects are often used in modern productions to make it scarier. Side-stepping the need for anything at all, the Ghost has been reinterpreted – as far back as the 18th century – as a hallucination, seen only by Macbeth, and so not actually present on stage.

THE AGE OF KINGS

The Age of Kings sequence would have had multiple layers of interpretation to Shakespeare's audience. Macbeth's desperation to remain king and the play's references to royal lineage can be tied together if you consider the Macbeths are childless – and, in some readings, have lost a child. There is no heir to the throne for King Macbeth, as there was not for Queen Elizabeth I – a much-discussed (but banned) topic during her long, virginal reign.

Macbeth says that the last image in the line of kings strongly resembles Banquo, but the sequence Shakespeare wrote was also intended to depict the lineage of King James VI of Scotland, by then the monarch of England too, and the patron of Shakespeare's theatre company.

Banquo's son, Fleance, is a small, often-cut character in the play. It's made famous for Banquo crying out *Fly, Fleance, fly!* as he tries to save his son from the murderers. Fleance does escape, and according to the Witches' prophecies is due to be king, although we never see or hear from him again. This happens a lot with minor characters in Shakespeare's plays, but considering the prophecy should king-to-be Fleance completely disappear when his father Banquo is murdered, or would it be interesting to have him reappear at the end of the play? What would that mean to Malcolm, soon to be crowned at Scone?

Historically, after defeating Macbeth, Malcolm began to raid England and expand his territory. If he hears of the prophecy about Fleance becoming king, perhaps Malcolm will encounter a similar struggle for power as Macbeth did. It's easy to imagine: Macbeth starts equivocating, becomes a tyrant, and everyone dies; when Malcolm starts equivocating with Macduff, it brings into question what life might be like after the play finishes, under Malcolm's reign.

THE MALCOLM SCENE

Malcolm's exchange with Macduff is an extended test of loyalty that ends with a powerful dramatic punch. Much rehearsal time is spent working out what a character's objective in each scene might be, and in what order characters enter, so perhaps the audience could be helped by a moment alone with Malcolm before Macduff arrives, as he somehow makes his intentions clear. Or perhaps the audience only see Malcolm being villainous, and are taken on the same journey as Macduff, believing Malcolm's lies until the end.

The later revelation of the slaughter of Macduff's family is hard to handle well and is sometimes considered poor writing, but it's a tremendously powerful scene when played well. It should be upsetting, shocking and heart-breaking. His grief is sometimes brushed over by Malcolm's following lines, and after the loyalty test, an unsympathetic Malcolm can make it hard for an audience to follow him as the rising hero-king.

Our foreknowledge of the Macduff family's fate should make Malcolm's *Why in that rawness left you Wife and Child?* an uncomfortable line to hear. Irrespective of whether or not we know he's testing Macduff, Malcolm did not witness the murders that we, the audience, sat through in the previous scene.

So it's not an easy part to play; if the audience is to like Malcolm, and his followers are to consider him a better deal as a leader than Macbeth, the actor playing Malcolm has to make a big impression in those brief early scenes as Duncan's son; then become a strategic philosopher with Macduff while appearing to be a despotic, megalomaniac liar; then finally transform into a leader of men and a presumptive good king.

THE FIGHTS

A number of productions have tried to stage part of the battle between Norway, the Scottish rebels and Duncan's army. Seeing him fight bravely and courageously, as we shortly afterwards hear him so reported, can be particularly useful in setting up the character of Macbeth.

Duncan's murder is hardly ever brought on stage, though it has been presented on film. It's a very different murder from anything Macbeth might have been used to in battle. There's something 'other' about murdering someone in their sleep, presumably covering their mouth with a hand; difficult to twist the dagger in under the ribcage to the heart – something personal and intimate – that's very different from fighting on a battlefield.

Plunging steel through thick furs and bedsheets, blood gushing up from a startled, betrayed look of surprise, might be easier to portray on film, if at all.

The off-stage murder of Lady Macduff and her son has been as horrifying as the off-stage rape and mutilation of Lavinia in Shakespeare's only classic revenge tragedy, *Titus Andronicus*. Macduff receiving the news (*What, all my pretty chickens?*) is a pitiful shimmer of King Lear kneeling next to the body of his daughter Cordelia.

So, too, the murder of Banquo and escape of Fleance, which has been staged in almost every order you can think of: whether Fleance sees his father murdered and tries to fight off one of the murderers before being ordered to run, or whether he flees while Banquo is fighting them off, perhaps even seeing his father begin to win. The last image Fleance has of that fight could be terribly poignant.

The final fight between antagonist and protagonist is the catharsis the audience has been waiting for, whether it's Edgar and Edmund in *King Lear*, or the duel between Hamlet and Laertes. The end of Macbeth and Macduff's fight takes place off-stage (very likely because on-stage decapitation isn't easy to fake), but hopefully a large part will have taken place on-stage before they exit. It's a fight that has a good journey for the audience en route to it, as we see Macbeth's confidence wane, and Macduff exacting his revenge on the man responsible for his family's bloody murder.

MORE THAN TEN...

As I've indicated earlier in this book, there's some extended metrical analysis that can be done. A lot of people disagree with the process, and it puts an incredible amount of faith both in the writer and those printing his works, none of whom were necessarily sober when they were creating.

However, it's a process that has helped me and others in the rehearsal room, so I'd suggest it's worth looking at the speeches in the DURING section to see if anything interesting comes up.

If Shakespeare had wanted a line of metre to be ten syllables long, he was skilled enough to make it so. If it's more than ten, there might be something to note about what the character is saying.

When there's more than ten syllables in a line of poetry, I've put a +1 or +2 next to the line:

MACBETH
First, as I am his kinsman and his subject,   **+1**

Here, the thought Macbeth is trying to convey tries to flow over the metrical line, but is restrained by it. Talking about his dual loyal status to his King must be difficult in the middle of a speech about regicide, so the metre wrinkles slightly, a clue to the actor about Macbeth's feelings at this point, and ultimately a piece of his character jigsaw puzzle.

Earlier in the speech, a thought changes in the middle of the metrical line:

MACBETH
If it were done when 'tis done, then 'twere well
It were **done quickly**: if th'Assassination   **+1**
Could trammel up the consequence, and catch

This is the first recorded use of the word *assassination* – Shakespeare seems to have created the word for this speech. By not using the more personal word *assassin*, which already existed, Macbeth distances himself from the idea of murder with the more abstract *assassination*.

The extra syllable wrinkles the metre, but the thought changing mid-line with the colon gives the actor a beat to breath. In terms of stage technique, the actor can pause before using the word for the first time, giving it weight; in terms of character, Macbeth can hesitate before speaking the word of murder.

TAKING YOUR EXPERIENCE FURTHER...

Everyone has their own opinion on how a Shakespeare play should be performed or produced. All the performance options and questions Shakespeare has left us, and how they have been met – or ignored – will directly affect your response to the play. Here are some of the main parameters.

THE USE OF THE SPACE

Partly dependent on the type of space the play was performed in (a theatre, a wood, a warehouse, or an old shopping mall…)

– Whether the audience was seated all around the stage, along two sides, or end-on to the performance, and whether the configuration intentionally creates sight-line issues (to obscure a piece of stage business)
– Whether parts of the set came from above or beneath the stage, or were moved on or off from the sides
– Whether the actors engaged with the audience, interacted with them or moved through them – in other words, whether the playing space and the auditorium were fused together, or kept distinct and separate

THE DESIGN

Different from how the space was used by the actors, the design of the show can place the play in a particular time or period to try to reflect a particular issue. It could be 16th-century Scotland, a modern-day council estate, the Second World War, or a 'non-place' that is harder to distinguish from the set, but perhaps indicated by costume from a particular period – formal military or army clothes, traditional Scottish kilts, or office suits.

– A non-space might rely on lighting effects to aid the location shift from the heath to the various castles
– Some productions can be prop-heavy, using lots of objects to help tell the story; some only use a single dagger and crown
– Considering the number of people who are killed, there could be a lot of stage-blood, or something else used to signify the idea of 'blood'
– Depending on where the camera or audience is in relation to Macbeth, Birnam wood coming to Dunsinane could be seen from Malcolm's perspective, Macbeth's point of view, or not at all

THE STRUCTURE

In terms of the overall aesthetic of the production, there are other things to consider. This is an oft-produced play, and extraordinary efforts are made to try to do something new with it. In recent productions, the first scene has been cut entirely, other scenes have been moved to different parts of the play, or repeated.

- Whether there was an interval, and if it felt well-placed – could it have come earlier?
- Whether any of the actors played more than one part. In smaller-scale productions, actors often double-up the parts they play, sometimes with interesting effects: Duncan can double with the Doctor; Ross with one of the Murderers; perhaps one of the Witches and Lady Macduff
- Whether many (or any) lines of text, or the order of the scenes were changed to tell the story in a different way. An account of which edition of the play was used is usually mentioned in the production's programme
- If something was cut, it could have been omitted to help make the production setting work better, or simply to make the running time shorter. This happens less with *Macbeth*, which is a fairly short play, but more commonly with *Hamlet*, whose full text would run to about four hours of performance

THE WITCHES
As discussed earlier, the room for interpretation in these parts is enormous.

- Sometimes the actors have pushed for funnier rather than scary Witches. In an RSC production in 2011 they were played by children, and by much older women at the Globe in 2010. A film in 2009 cast them as siren-like beautiful seductresses, and a more recent production had them as medical nurses, torturing other characters in a hospital
- The Witches are only written into three scenes, but considering how powerful their presence can be, there have been productions keeping them onstage throughout the play, or which have periodically brought them onstage to watch or influence the action. Others stick to the text, having them only appear in the scenes where they speak
- With modern theatrical technology at a production's disposal, any number of special effects (smoke, digital projections, or puppetry) have been used in the Witches' scenes to make them scarier

THE PORTER
In the past he has been played many different ways – as an alcoholic, a forgetful old man, and as a stand-up comic improvising with the audience around his lines.

- It's a character that has been getting younger over the last few decades of productions. A young man – or woman – will bring a completely different type of gravitas to the scene than an older actor
- Has the actor managed to make these tricky lines funny? Or does the comedy come more from improvised, non-verbal interaction with the audience, carrying a bottle of alcohol or a piss-bucket, clearing up from the night's celebrations?

- Similar to the Witches, the part is open for an unscripted late return after his main scene – perhaps doubling the part, and combining it with the servant-character Seyton

THE ENDING

How you end a dark, tragic drama is a difficult question, and every production will be different.

- The standard twentieth-century close is a slow fade out of the lights to black, often with solemn drums
- The ending that Shakespeare's audience might have expected – a celebratory, music-and-dance ending
- But if you're reading the play – how would *you* end it?

LIKE OR UNLIKE

If you were experiencing the play for the first time –

- Did you think it was going to be difficult to understand? And was it?
- Did the production you see change the ideas you had about the play, whether they were good or bad?
- And … would you go and see it again?

WHERE TO SPRING NEXT...?

You've experienced one of Shakespeare's greatest and bloodiest tragedies, so what now?

If you've been reading the play
- buy a different edition of the play, and read a different editor's introduction notes
- go to see a staged production
- watch a film version

If you've seen a production
- watch another production of the same play; see how it differs
- read – or re-read – the text; see which bits were left out and bring together your memories of the performance with the script in front of you: perhaps some lines or scenes were cut, considered too difficult to understand, or they didn't fit with the director's vision of the play; can you see why the actor, director and designers made the decisions they made?

Perhaps dive into another Shakespeare play
- another tragedy, perhaps *King Lear* (an epic play filled with madness, blinding and torture) or *Othello* (an examination of absolute love, passion and jealousy)
- head to *Henry V,* Shakespeare's historical account of the Boy Who Would Be King as he rises to lead his country and claim back France, or *Richard II,* one of his most poetically beautiful plays, with the tragic fall of the King Who Would Be Boy
- the mistaken-identity almost-farce of *The Comedy of Errors*, or the lovers, fairies and forestry sexual shenanigans of *A Midsummer Night's Dream*, both with a dark heart hidden at their core

You have a selection of thirty-nine plays in all, offering an exploration of the human heart and mind in ways that are quite starkly different from each other, whether you're reading them, watching them in a theatre or on screen, yet all linked by one writer, his imagination, and his rather deft ability with the quill.

I've listed some books, films, theatres and companies below. Anything mentioned will point you in many different directions in the recent Shakespeare-related world.

It all depends where you'd like to spring next...

SPRINGBOARDS

Below, some carefully chosen *Macbeth*-related Books, Films and Websites to consider.

PRINT

Macbeth (Arden Shakespeare, 1962)
Edited by the literary scholar and author Kenneth Muir, he focuses his introduction looking at which parts of the play were written by Shakespeare. The notes (see the Guide to Other Texts, below) are comprehensive, and have a strong literary-critical bent.

The Player's Shakespeare Macbeth (Heinemann, 1962)
Edited by a former headteacher, the thoughtful notes by J. H. Walter are full of staging and dramatic interpretive readings and questions.

A Shakespeare Miscellany (Penguin, 2005)
David and Ben Crystal's coffee-table quiz-book of facts about Shakespeare's life, language and plays, together with descriptions of Elizabethan life and theatre, quotes from well-known Shakespeare actors, and anecdotes of modern film and theatre productions of the plays.

The Northern Lights (Scholastic, 1995)
Philip Pullman's other-Earth magic-realism tale, filled with ghosts, witches, familiars, a man mad for power, and a woman mad with darkness.

The RSC Shakespeare: The Complete Works (Palgrave Macmillan, 2008)
A recent edition of Shakespeare's works closely based on the First Folio. Edited by the literary scholars Jonathan Bate and Eric Rasmussen, with notes suggesting staging possibilities of each scene.

The Oxford Companion to Shakespeare (OUP, 2005)
Stanley Wells and Michael Dobson's straightforward and well laid-out play-by-play companion to Shakespeare's works, life and times.

Contested Will (James Shapiro, Faber, 2010)
A detective-like analysis of the conspiracy theories surrounding the authorship of the plays and poems, by the American scholar James Shapiro, accounting the various (slightly mad) historical figures' fascination with the author responsible for the plays written under the name of Shakespeare.

GUIDE TO OTHER TEXTS OF THE PLAY

If you decide to move on to an edited text of the play it will be probably be filled with notes, either below the text, to the side, or at the back of the book. Years of study and editing have crammed these plays with commentary, asides and questions.

NOTES

They can be daunting to look at if you're not used to them. Many will tell you what a word means, or that there's an allusion to the Bible, but depending on when it was written there may not be a reason given as to why the character might have chosen that particular word, or what it could mean to them or the audience that a biblical reference was made.

Also, names like Theobald or Malone may appear from time to time, referring to earlier editors of the plays. The interpretations and textual emendations they once suggested are often provided.

F VS Q

Some notes will refer to words or spellings as being F or Q1, Q2, etc – which means the spellings taken from the Folio, the First Quarto printing, the Second Quarto printing, etc. This won't bother you much in *Macbeth*, since the play appeared only in Folio, but the Quarto versus Folio discussions surrounding *Hamlet* or *King Lear* draw a lot of attention.

NAMES AND STAGE DIRECTIONS

Some will supplement the sparse Folio stage directions with full locations and descriptions of what the characters may be doing, which are either implied in the text or based on the editor's interpretation.

Character names vary too – presenting Lady instead of Lady Macbeth. And the spelling of names can vary too, with Rosse, Lenox and Hecat versus Ross, Lennox and Hecate, but these are all idiosyncratic, and shouldn't be misleading.

'QUIBBLING'

Macbeth, at one point, says

Here comes my fit again, else I might have been perfect

Some editors write that *perfect* is a 'quibble' on *fit*, depending on how you pronounce it; in other words, there's a form of language play taking place, either by Shakespeare or by someone interpreting it that way. Still, finding a reason as to why the character might choose to play with words at that point – to make a joke, perhaps – is the point.

FILM

Fight Club (1999) – David Fincher's brilliant, terrifying, psychotic, deranged exploration of madness through insomnia; recommended with a strong caution to young viewers for the adult content – *Macbeth* has no censorship over it, but *Fight Club* is certified by the BBFC for viewers over the age of 18.

Lost Highway (1997) – Equally, David Lynch's films are like mad dreams, and this one deals with a man who actually becomes someone else, so unable is his brain to cope with the thought of having murdered someone.

Macbeth (1983) – part of the BBC's complete works collection, with Nicol Williamson and Jane Lapotaire. Dated, and has a low-budget feel to it, but like the rest of the series, it's a raw, terrific, shabby, classic.

A Performance of Macbeth (1979) – directed by Trevor Nunn, and based on his Other Place production at the RSC, with Ian McKellen and Judi Dench. Generally regarded as one of the finest – and scariest – productions of *Macbeth* for the last 50 years.

Maqbool (2003) – *Macbeth* meets *The Godfather* in present-day Mumbai. Some of the finest modern Shakespeare productions have come from non-English language translations of the plays; talking of which ...

Kumonosu-jô aka *Throne of Blood* (1957) – legendary director Akira Kurosawa's adaptation of *Macbeth*. Shakespeare is timeless, universal and Samurai.

Scarface (1983) – a very graphic drug-, gun- and blood-fuelled account of a modern-day American gangster played in an award-winning role by Al Pacino, whose stratospheric, murderous rise and fall is a nod to Shakespeare's *Macbeth*. Again, recommended with a strong caution to young viewers for the adult content – *Macbeth* has no censorship over it, but *Scarface* is certified by the BBFC for viewers over the age of 18.

WEB
Pointing towards Shakespeare theatre companies or excellent online media resources.

The British Library – www.bl.uk
List, view scans, and compare 107 different copies of the 21 plays printed in Quarto before the theatre closures of 1642.

Bell Shakespeare Company – www.bellshakespeare.com.au
A leading Australian Shakespeare company, based out of Sydney, with a terrific education programme.

The Folger Library – www.folger.edu
The largest collection of Shakespeare material in the world, located in Washington DC.

The National School of Drama Theatre Festival Delhi – www.nsdtheatrefest.com
Held over two weeks every January in Delhi, often featuring over half a dozen productions or (usually fairly radical) adaptations of Shakespeare plays.

Play Shakespeare – www.playshakespeare.com
An excellent free-to-use collection of Shakespeare's works, reviews of productions and books, together with a broad online community, allowing festivals and companies across the world to network. Builders of the iPhone Shakespeare App.

The Royal Shakespeare Company – www.rsc.org.uk
Three newly refurbished theatres with an ensemble company playing year-round in Shakespeare's home town. The website has a great deal of audio and visual interviews and clips of productions.

The Shakespeare Institute – http://www.birmingham.ac.uk/Shakespeare
The internationally renowned research institution, established to 'push the boundaries of knowledge about Shakespeare studies and Renaissance drama'.

Shakespeare's Globe – www.shakespearesglobe.org
The reconstructed Shakespeare's Globe Theatre, London, with details both of their main summer theatre season, and their extraordinary winter education season.

Shakespeare's Globe, Neuss – www.shakespeare-festival.de/en
A replica of Shakespeare's Globe in Neuss, Germany, with a fine festival of plays and a regular receiver of visiting Shakespeare companies.

Shakespeare's Words – www.shakespeareswords.com
The website based on the Shakespeare's Words Glossary and Language Companion, free to use: linguistically explore Shakespeare's works like never before. The Glossary at the back of this book is adapted from the Shakespeare Words database.

Stratford Shakespeare Festival – www.stratfordfestival.ca
Based out of Stratford, Canada, a highly renowned theatre company with wide-ranging season respected throughout North America.

Yukio Ninagawa – www.ninagawastudio.net
His company – together with British producers Thelma Holt and the RSC – have been bringing Ninagawa's especial brand of Shakespeare production to the UK since the 1990s. Often thematically expansive, and regularly featuring highly regarded Noh and Kabuki actors.

A SHORT SPRINGBOARD INTO ...

Romeo and Juliet

A tragic tale of family feuds, young love, street fights, bloodshed, and a kiss at a dance.

....

☞ ROMEO

The tragic male lead doesn't have the best reputation. Actors, audience and scholars alike often think of him as being drab, wet, and a moaner – a kind of teen, puberty-ridden Hamlet.

Played well, he can be a fascinating foil to Juliet. He's older than Juliet, but boys often hit puberty later than girls, so in terms of their sexual awakening, they could be equally matched, but we don't see them go through the same life experiences.

Romeo believes he's been in love before; the play begins with him broken-hearted and obsessed with a girl called Rosalind, but Juliet has never been in love before. So on the one hand we're offered a character pure and utterly naive; on the other, we have someone who thinks they've known love, until he really, actually does fall in love. Both are familiar, fascinating things to watch unfold.

While Juliet is trying to deal with being forced into an arranged marriage, Romeo has to grow up incredibly fast too, in a different way: his best friend is murdered in front of him, and he very quickly becomes a murderer too, immediately avenging Mercutio's death.

Juliet then has to accept that her husband has killed her cousin, and that he will be exiled. A lot to cope with in your first year as a teenager.

....

☞ JULIET'S AGE

It's almost entirely impossible you'll see the leads cast to their ages. From what the Nurse says, Juliet is around 13 years old. Romeo is around 16.

Exactly why Shakespeare wanted to examine love at that age – an age where adults tend to say, *You're too young to know what love is* – is unknown, although young marriage was more common in his time, when lifespan was generally shorter.

Certainly, watching love blossom with two young, naive people is a very different experience from a Romeo and Juliet who are clearly in their late teens or early twenties (and so very probably sexually experienced). He explored love between older characters in other plays: he wanted this love to be pure, and full, and unadulterated.

Interestingly, Juliet is given 12½ lines when she wakes up in the tomb, before she kills herself: one for each year she lived.

○ SPEECH   MERCUTIO and QUEEN MAB

Romeo meets with his friends, and begins to tell them of a bad dream he had. One of his friends, Mercutio, has a long speech about Queen Mab, a Father Christmas-like Faerie that speeds around at night, dropping dreams into people's heads.

In the First Folio, the speech is set in prose, with the last four lines in verse; modern editions often re-set the text as verse throughout, but the Folio structure gives a lovely notion of Mercutio improvising his wild story in prose, switching up into verse as he appears to get emotional and carried away, before Romeo brings him back down to earth with his *thou talk'st of nothing! True* Mercutio replies calmly, *I talk of dreams...*

☞ ROMEO and JULIET MEET

An English sonnet has 14 lines, with an *abab cdcd efef gg* rhyme scheme. Such is the wonder of their first meeting (see BEFORE, p.12), so heavily do they immediately fall in love, Shakespeare has them share a sonnet.

What's more, the encounter is 18 lines long: so it's such a wonderful moment, they actually immediately begin to share *another* sonnet as they kiss for the first time. But they don't get to finish the second sonnet, and are interrupted as Juliet is taken away by her nurse.

That true love found and sonnet left unfinished makes Romeo leave his friends, scale a wall, risk being beaten, and find Juliet once more...

☞ THE DEATH OF YOUTH

Halfway through the play, Mercutio and Tybalt have died. By the end of the play, Benvolio and Romeo's Man are the only members of the young generation still standing.

Through Romeo and Juliet's tragedy, an entire generation is wiped from the slate; the feud between the Capulets and Montagues has left them with status as their heirs, and (unless they try to have more children – which is unlikely at their age) the ends of their family lines.

GLOSSARY

abhorred horrifying

abide stay

absolute[1] curt [*with an* ~ *'Sir, not I'*]

absolute[2] total [*I built an* ~ *trust; in* ~ *fear of you*]

abuse deceive

accompt reckoning

act performance *or* action

adage saying

addition[1] distinction [*he does receive particular* ~]

addition[2] title [*Thane of Cawdor, in which* ~, *hail*]

address'd prepared

adhere suit

admir'd amazing

advantage right moment

afeard afraid

affection state of mind

affeer'd confirmed

ague fever

alarum call to arms *or* attack

all-thing completely

amend get better

angel spirit

angerly angrily

annoyance injury

anon soon

antic bizarre

apace quickly

apart away from here

appoint decide

approve prove

argument subject

arm'd furnished with arms *or* armour

aroynt, aroint be gone

art skill *or* knowledge

artificial produced by magic

assay attempt

assurance certainty

attempt attack [*prepares for some* ~ *of war*]

attend[1] go with [*better health* ~ *his Majesty; the illness should* ~ *it*]

attend[2] await [*censures* ~ *the true event; I would* ~ *his leisure;* ~ *those men our pleasure?*]

auger-hole tiny spot

aught anything

augures, augurs prophecies

authoris'd vouched for

avaunt go away

avouch[1] justify [*bid my will* ~ *it*]

avouch[2] declare [*this which he avouches*]

aweary tired

aye always

badged stained

baited tormented

balls golden orbs [*two-fold* ~ *and treble sceptres carry*]

bane ruin

bank coast

bark ship

battle battalion [*lead our first* ~]

become[1] befit [*I dare do all that may* ~ *a man; well* ~ *a woman's story*]

become[2] honour [*so well thy words* ~ *thee*]

before[1] ahead [*thou art so far* ~]

before[2] in front [*had he his hurts* ~*?*]

beguile deceive
beldams old hags
bellman bell-ringer for an impending death
bend up exert
benison blessing
bent determined
bestow'd lodged
bestride stand over
betimes at an early hour, soon
betray's deceive us
bid ask
bill list
birthdom native land
bladed with many shoots [*~ corn*]
blaspheme slander
blast storm [*striding the ~*]
blasted withered *or* cursed [*this ~ heath*]
bleeding blood-soaked [*the ~ and the grim alarm*]
blind-worm slow-worm
blood kinship [*the near in ~*]
blood-bolter'd with hair matted with blood
bloody bloodsoaked, bloodthirsty
bodements omens
bond pledge
boot, to as well
borne in hand deceived
bosom[1] intimate [*our ~ interest*]
bosom[2] inner person [*my ~ franchis'd*]
botches blemishes
brainsickly foolishly
brave noble
bravely splendidly
break reveal [*~ this enterprise to me*]
breast heart
breath utterance [*deep, mouth-honour, ~*]
breech'd covered
breed lineage [*blaspheme his ~*]

brew'd ready to appear
brinded streaked
broad[1] widespread [*as ~ and general as the casing air; honours deep and ~*]
broad[2] candid [*~ words*]
broil turmoil
brows[1] appearance [*the ~ of grace*]
brows[2] forehead [*pull your hat upon your ~*]
bruited reported

cabin'd shut up as in a small room
call'd reckoned [*how far is't ~ to Forres?*]
card compass-card [*th'shipman's ~*]
careless uncared-for
casing surrounding [*general as the ~ air*]
cast throw down [*I made a shift to ~ him*]
cast the water inspect the urine
catalogue roll-call
catch seize [*~ with his surcease, success; ~ the nearest way*]
cause business [*we shall have ~ of State*]
censures opinions
cestern cistern, water-tank
chair me keep me on the throne
challenge reproach
chamber bedroom
chamberlain bedroom attendant
champion challenge [*~ me to th'utterance*]
chance event [*an hour before this ~*]
chaps chops, jaws
charg'd burdened
charge[1] duty [*mock their ~ with snore; an imperial ~*]
charge[2] command [*I ~ you*]
charmed enchanted [*~ pot*]
charnel-house burial vault

chaudron entrails

cheer kind welcome [*you do not give the ~; receive what ~ you may*]

cherubins cherubim, angels

chid scolded

choke smother

choppy rough

chough jackdaw

chuck chick

clear[1] faultless [*so ~ in his great office*]

clear[2] blameless [*keep my bosom franchis'd, and allegiance ~*]

clear[3] cheerfully [*look up ~*]

clearness freedom from suspicion

clept called

cling shrivel [*till famine ~ thee*]

clogs hinders

cloister'd confined

clos'd contained

close[1] concealed [*the ~ contriver of all harms*]

close[2] near [*stand ~*]

close[3] combine again [*she'll ~, and be herself*]

closet cabinet

cloudy sullen [*the ~ messenger*]

coign projecting corner

colours standard-bearers [*drums and ~*]

combustion tumult

come what come may whatever happens

commend[1] entrust [*I do ~ you to their backs; Justice ~s th' ingredience of our poison'd chalice to our own lips*]

commend[2] praise [*I ~ your pains*]

commission authority

compass'd surrounded

compose produce

composition truce

compt, in held in trust

compunctious remorseful

concluded decided

conference conversation

confineless boundless

confusion destruction

conjure ask solemnly

consent opinion

consider ponder

constancy determination, resolution

construction interpretation

contend struggle *or* compete

content happiness

contented agreeable

continent self-controlled

contriver schemer

convey carry on secretly

convince overcome

cool'd become cold with fear

copy tenure, copying

corporal physical

countenance confront

counterfeit false imitation

cours'd pursued

course attack by dogs [*I must fight the ~*]

cracks explosive charges

crave beg

crests helmets

cribb'd shut up as in a tiny hovel

cross'd afflicted

crown to the toe head to foot

curs mastiffs

curriers messengers

custom habit

cyme plant-top *or* senna, drug to cause vomiting

dainty particular [*let us not be ~ of leave-taking*]

dame lady

dareful full of defiance

deadly death-like

deepest weightiest [*in ~ consequence*]

defect deficiency
degrees ranks
delicate delightful [*the air is ~*]
deliver report *or* describe
demi-wolves dog/wolf cross-breeds
design purpose
dew water
diminitive diminutive
directly at once
direful dreadful
direness terror
disasters misfortunes
discomfort discouragement
discovery spying
disjoint fall to pieces
dismal disastrous
dispatch[1] direction [*put this night's great business into my ~*]
dispatch[2] be quick [*come, sir, dispatch*]
dispatch'd finished off
displaced removed
disposition natural temperament
dispute it deal with it
disseat remove from the throne
distance enmity [*such bloody ~*]
distemper'd insane
distracted agitated
ditch-deliver'd born in a ditch
divers several
division variation
do, I'll I'll do harm
doff get rid of
dolour sorrow
doom doomsday
doubt fear [*I ~, some danger does approach you*]
doubtful fearful
downfall downfallen
downy soft as down, comfort-giving
drab slut
dread terrifying
drenched full of drink

dudgeon hilt
dunnest darkest

earnest pledge
ecstasy[1] frenzy [*restless ~*]
ecstasy[2] emotion [*violent sorrow seems a modern ~*]
effect result *or* sign
eminence special honour
endure allow [*~ our setting-down*]
enow enough
epicure pleasure-seeker
equivocation double-meaning
equivocator dealer in double meanings
estate[1] kingdom [*we will establish our ~ upon our eldest*]
estate[2] situation [*th' ~ of the world*]
eterne for ever
event outcome [*the true ~*]
Evil, the the King's evil, scrofula
excite stir up [*~ the mortified man*]
execution slaughter [*bloody ~*]
expectation expected guests
expedition speedy action

fact crime [*damned ~*]
faculties powers
fain gladly
faith-breach treason
false[1] sham [*~ face*]
false[2] treacherous [*~ heart; ~ thanes*]
false[3] wrongly [*if thou speak'st ~*]
false[4] faithlessly [*play ~*]
fancies imaginings
fantastical unreal
farrow litter of pigs
fatal full of doom
father, good venerable sir
favour[1] pardon [*give me your ~*]
favour[2] appearance [*to alter ~*]
fee'd hired

fee-grief individual sorrow
fell terrible [~ *cruelty;* ~ *purpose*]
fell of hair hair on my skin
fenny fen-living
field field of battle
file[1] list [*the valu' ~d; a ~ of all the gentry*]
file[2] rank of soldiers [*a station in the ~*]
fil'd defiled
first start [*their ~ of manhood*]
first and last, at to one and all
firstling first fruits
fit attack [*then comes my ~ again; the ~ is momentary*]
fitful full of fits
fits turmoil [*~ o'th' season*]
flaws gusts
flighty swiftly conceived [*the ~ purpose*]
flout insult
foisons abundance
forc'd strengthened
fork forked tongue [*adder's ~*]
forsworn perjured
founded secure
fountain source
frailties bodies
frame framework
franchis'd free from evil
free[1] frank [*let us speak our ~ hearts each to other*]
free[2] freely [*which else should ~ have wrought*]
free[3] enjoyed in freedom [*receive ~ honours*]
friend, to friendly
fry offspring
fume harmful vapour
furbish'd shining *or* refurbished

gall bile
gallowglasses axe-wielding Irish soldiers

genius attendant spirit
gentle[1] peaceful [*ere humane statute purg'd the ~ weal*]
gentle[2] refined [*our ~ senses*]
gentle[3] noble [*~ lady*]
gentle[4] kind [*~ Heavens*]
gently without a fight
germen seed
get beget [*thou shalt ~ kings*]
gild smear
gin snare
'gins begins
gives out proclaims
glass crystal ball
gloss deceptive appearance
go off die
goodness benefit [*the chance of ~*]
goose smoothing iron [*you may roast your ~*]
goose look stupid face
gospell'd converted to the gospel
gouts drops
grac'd stately [*the ~ person of our Banquo*]
gracious godly [*the ~ Duncan*]
grandam grandmother
grave respected [*your good advice (which still hath been both ~ and prosperous)*]
gripe grip
grooms servants
guise custom
gulf huge stomach

half-world hemisphere
harbinger herald
harness armour
harp'd guessed
haunt visit often [*where they most breed and ~*]
having fortune [*great prediction of noble ~*]

hawk'd at pursued
heaviest saddest [*the ~ sound*]
heavily sadly [*the tidings, which I have ~ borne*]
heavy[1] serious [*~ judgement; ~ summons*]
heavy[2] pressing [*the sin of my ingratitude even now was ~ on me*]
heavy[3] brutal [*~ hand*]
hedge-pig hedgehog
hell-kite hellish savage
hereafter at some time in the future
here-approach arrival here
here-remain stay
hermits people who pray for someone
hie hurry
highly ambitiously [*what thou wouldst ~*]
home fully [*trusted ~*]
hose breeches
housekeeper housedog
howlet young owl
humane civil [*~ statute*]
hums says 'hum'
husbandry thrift

'ild us reward us [*bid God ~ for your pains*]
ill bad
ill-compos'd made up of wicked elements
illness wickedness
image embodiment [*the great doom's ~*]
imperfect unclear [*you ~ speakers*]
impress force into service
incarnadine turn blood-red
informs takes form
ingredience ingredients
initiate novice [*the ~ fear*]
insane causing madness [*have we eaten on the ~ root*]

instruments[1] means [*the ~; wh⟨ wrought with them*]
instruments[2] weapons [*the Power above put on their ~*]
intent intention
interdiction prohibition
intermission delay
intrenchant uncuttable
invention fabrication
issue[1] offspring [*pray for this goo⟨ man, and for his ~; the truest issue ⟨ thy throne*]
issue[2] outcome [*certain ~ strokes mu⟨ arbitrate*]

jealousies suspicions
jocund joyful
juggling deceiving
jump risk [*we'd ~ the life to come*]
just[1] exact [*to the direction ~*]
just[2] exactly [*~ censures*]
jutty projection

kerns lightly armed Irish foot-soldie⟨
kites birds of prey

lapp'd wrapped
large generous [*be ~ in mirth*]
last final test [*I will try the ~*]
latch catch
lated overtaken by the night
lave wash
lavish impetuous [*~ spirit*]
leave leave-taking
leavy leafy, covered with foliage
lees dregs
lie, giving the deceiving *or* makir⟨ urinate
lighted shown the way
like equal [*yell'd out ~ syllable dolour*]
like, most very likely

limbeck distilling apparatus
lime birdlime
limited appointed [*'tis my ~ service*]
line strengthen [*~ the rebel with hidden help*]
linen pale [*~ cheeks*]
list, the combat arena
lodg'd flattened [*though bladed corn be ~*]
loon rogue
luxurious lecherous

magot-pie magpie
mansionry place of habitation
martlet house-martin
masterdom supremacy
mated astounded
maw belly
measure, in in due proportion
meet right and proper [*'tis most ~*]
memorise make memorable
mere complete [*the ~ lees; the ~ despair of surgery*]
mere own personal property [*of your ~*]
metaphysical supernatural
mettle temperament
minion favourite
ministers messengers
minutely taking place minute by minute
mischief catastrophe
moe more
mock deceive [*~ the time with fairest show*]
modern everyday [*violent sorrow seems a ~ ecstasy*]
more and less men of high and low rank
more-having acquiring
mortal[1] deadly [*~ thoughts*]
mortal[2] everyday [*~ custom*]

mortified dead to feeling
motives inspirations
mouth-honour honour shown in words not deeds
multitudinous innumerable
murther murder
murthers deadly wounds
muse wonder

napkins handkerchieves
natural touch normal feelings of affection
naught wicked
nave navel
navigation shipping
nearest closest to the throne [*those whose places are the ~*]
near'st most closely affecting [*my ~ of life*]
nerves sinews
nice detailed [*too ~, and yet too true*]
niggard miser
nigh near
nimbly bracingly
nonpareil person without equal
Norweyan Norwegian
note list [*the ~ of expectation*]
notion mind

occasion course of events
off'rings rituals
office[1] role [*his great ~*]
office[2] task [*unfelt sorrow is an ~ which the false man does easy*]
offices servants' quarters
old plenty of [*he should have ~ turning the key*]
ope open
other otherwise [*who dares receive it ~*]
out, were were in rebellion
o'erbear overwhelm
overcome suddenly come over

o'erfraught overburdened
o'erleap leap over [*I must fall down, or else ~*]
o'erleaps leaps too far over [*ambition, which ~ itself*]
over-red cover over with blood
o'ertook achieved
ow'd owned

paddock toad
pale pale-hearted [*that great bond which keeps me ~*]
pall wrap
palter quibble
parley meeting
parricide murder of a father
parted departed this life [*they say he ~ well*]
pass'd gone over [*~ in probation with you*]
passion[1] fit of anger [*you shall offend him, and extend his ~*]
passion[2] outburst [*this noble ~*]
patch fool
pauser delayer
peak waste away
pendent dangling
penthouse like a lean-to shed
perchance perhaps
perfect[1] well aware [*in your state of honour I am ~*]
perfect[2] totally content [*which in his death were ~; I had else been ~*]
pester'd troubled
physic medicine
physics cures
pious[1] loyal [*in ~ rage*]
pious[2] holy [*the most ~ Edward*]
pit-fall bird-trap
places ranks [*those whose ~ are the nearest*]
point sword-point [*~ against ~*]

point, at a in readiness, prepared, armed
portable endurable
possess inform
posset restorative hot drink
post courier
posterity descendants
posters fast travellers
power[1] authority [*none can call our ~ to accompt*]
power[2] armed force [*our ~ is ready, the English ~ is near*]
Powers gods [*merciful ~*]
prate prattle
predominance ascendancy
presently at once
pretence plan
pretend intend
pride of place highest point of flight
probation demonstration
procreant for the purpose of procreation
profound with secret powers
proof tested strength [*Bellona's bridegroom, lapp'd in ~*]
proper stuff complete nonsense
proportion weighing up
prosperous profitable [*your good advice (which still hath been both grave and ~)*]
protest affirm
pull in bring to a halt
purveyor one sent ahead to make preparations
push crisis [*this ~ will cheer me ever*]
put upon ascribe to

quarry heap of dead
quarters directions
quell murder
quoth said

rancours bitter feelings
rarer more unusual [~ *monsters*]
ravell'd tangled
ravin'd glutted
ravin up devour voraciously
rawness unprotected state
raze out erase
rebuk'd repressed
reckon with take full account of what is owed to
recoil fall away
reflection turning back [*the sun 'gins his ~*]
relation report [*O ~, too nice, and yet too true*]
relations relationships [*understood ~*]
relish trace
remembrance¹ attention [*let your ~ apply to Banquo*]
remembrance² memory [*my young ~*]
remembrancer reminder
render'd surrendered
requited repaid
resolv'd decided
ronyon mangy creature
rooky filled with rooks
round¹ crown [*the golden ~*]
round² circle dance [*your antic ~*]
rouse startle from a lair
rubs roughnesses
rugged¹ frowning [~ *looks*]
rugged² shaggy [*the ~ Russian bear*]
rule proper discipline [*the belt of ~*]

sad downcast
safe¹ certain [*But Banquo's safe?*]
safe² trustworthily [*doing everything ~*]
safety prudent course of action
sainted saintly
saucy insolent
scann'd examined

scap'd escaped
scarf up blindfold
school control [~ *yourself*]
scorch'd gashed
score account [*paid his ~*]
scour clear out
scruples¹ suspicions [*the black ~*]
scruples² doubts [*fears and ~ shake us*]
seat situation [*this castle hath a pleasant ~*]
seated firmly placed
secret magical [*you ~, black, and midnight hags*]
security over-confidence
seeling concealing
self-abuse self-deception
senna shrub which can cause vomiting
sennight week
sensible perceptible
sere withered
service table preparations
setting down siege
several¹ different [*each ~ crime*]
several² various [*your ~ loves*]
sewer chief servant
shadow conceal [*we ~ the numbers of our host*]
shag-hair'd having shaggy hair
shard-born born in dung
shift stratagem [*I made a ~ to cast him*]
shift away slip off
shipwracking causing shipwreck
shoughs shaggy-haired Icelandic dogs
show pretence [*mock the time with fairest ~*]
shut up end up
sightless invisible
single¹ slight [*poor and ~ business*]
single² particular [*my ~ state of man*]

skipping runaway [*these ~ Kernes*]
skirr scour
slab congealed
sleave strands
sleights trickeries
slipp'd failed to keep
slips sprigs [*~ of yew*]
sliver'd cut off
smok'd gave off bloody steam
society[1] companions [*mingle with ~*]
society[2] companionship [*make ~ the sweeter welcome*]
sold as if for sale
soldiership soldierly qualities
sole mere [*whose ~ name blisters our tongues*]
solely entirely [*give ~ sovereign sway*]
solicits prevails upon
something somewhat [*~ from the palace*]
sooth true
sore violent [*this ~ night*]
sorely heavily [*the heart is ~ charg'd*]
sorry sad [*this is a ~ sight*]
soul, half a halfwit
speak proclaim [*~ him full of grace*]
speculation power of knowing
speeches conversation
spongy drunken
sprites[1] feelings [*cheer we up his ~*]
sprites[2] ghosts [*from your graves rise up, and walk like ~*]
spurn scorn
spy chance to spy
stableness stability
staff rod of office [*give me my ~*]
stamp stamped coin
stand continue [*it should not ~ in thy posterity*]
stand to come forward
stand to't get down to business
staunchless insatiable

start[1] jump [*why do you ~; senses to recoil and ~*]
start[2] startle [*direness ... cannot once ~ me*]
start[3] burst from sockets [*~, eyes*]
starting startled reaction
starts outbursts [*these flaws and ~*]
state[1] chair of state [*our hostess keeps her ~*]
state[2] position [*in your ~ of honour*]
staves spears
stay await [*a crew of wretched souls, that ~ his cure*]
stick pierce [*our fears in Banquo ~ deep*]
sticking-place place where something is held fast
stir stirring *or* rouse
straight at once [*I'll call upon you ~*]
strangely-visited extremely afflicted
strangles quenches
striding sitting astride
strokes blows
studied learned by heart
stuff nonsense [*O proper ~*]
stuff'd clogged [*the ~ bosom*]
suborn'd bribed
sudden unpredictable [*false, deceitful ~, malicious*]
suffer perish [*both the worlds ~*]
suggestion temptation
suits matches
summer-seeming befitting summer time
supp'd had supper
surcease completion
surfeited overfilled
surmise imagining
sway power [*sovereign ~ an masterdom*]
sway by am controlled by
swears makes promises [*one that and lies*]

swelling magnificent [*prologues to the ~ act*]
swelter'd oozing
swinish like pigs

taint become weak [*I cannot ~ with fear*]
taints faults [*~ and blames*]
taking-off removal
tarrying staying
teems brings forth
temperate calm
tend on wait upon
tending care
thane Scottish lord
thick-coming frequently appearing
thickens grows dim, darken
thought, upon a in a moment
thoughts intentions [*mortal ~*]
thralls slaves
time society [*to beguile the ~*]
titles dominions
tooth fangs [*danger of her former ~*]
top, to to surpass
touch quality [*he wants the natural ~*]
towering soaring
trace follow on from [*all unfortunate souls that ~ him in his line*]
trains stratagems
trammel up catch up, as in a net
transpose alter
treatise story
trenched deep
trifled made trivial
try fight out [*I will ~ the last*]
tugg'd battered

unbend weaken
undeeded without any deeds performed
unfelt not experienced
unkindness ingratitude

unknown to not had sex with
unlineal not of the same family
unmake destroy
unmannerly inappropriately
unnatural monstrous [*~ deeds*]
unrough unbearded
unsanctified wicked
unseam'd split in two
unsex me take away my sex
unspeak take back
untimely prematurely
untitled with no right to rule
uproar throw into turmoil
use custom [*against the ~ of nature*]
utterance, to th' to the bitter end

valu'd discriminating [*the ~ file*]
vantage¹ right moment [*the Norweyan Lord, surveying ~*]
vantage² advantage [*hidden help and ~*]
vap'rous misty
vault sky
venture risky enterprise
verities truth *or* truths
virtue capability
vizards masks
vouch'd praised

wait on accompany [*you ~ Nature's mischief*]
wake urge [*to ~ Northumberland*]
want need
wanton flourishing [*joys, ~ in fulness*]
warrant authorisation
warranted justified
wassail carousal
wasteful destructive
watch signal, watchword, call [*whose howl's his ~*]
watch'd kept vigil
watchers people who stay wide-awake

watching wakefulness
water-rugs rough-haired water-dogs
weal state
wear possess [~ *thou thy wrongs*]
weigh'd balanced
whey-face pasty-face
whole intact [~ *as the marble*]
wholesome in good condition
will desire [*our ~ became the servant to defect*]
wound up prepared for action
wink fail to look
wit mental sharpness

witness evidence
womanly feeble
wonders feelings of wonder
wooingly enticingly
worm snake
wrought carried out *or* acted upon
wrack wreck *or* ruin
written preserved
wrongs wrong-doings

yawning sleep-inducing
yesty foaming
young inexperienced

CHARACTERS

Location: Scotland, aside from the scene between Malcolm and Macduff at the end of Act 4, which is set in England

SCOTTISH COURT
DUNCAN, King of Scotland*
DONALBAIN*
MALCOLM   His sons

GENERALS OF THE KING'S ARMY
MACBETH, (Thane of GLAMIS; later, Thane of CAWDOR; later still, KING of Scotland
MACDUFF, Thane of FIFE
BANQUO

NOBLEMEN OF SCOTLAND
LENOX*
ROSS*
MENTETH*
ANGUS*
CATHNESS*

OTHERS
LADY MACDUFF

FLEANCE, Son to Banquo
BOY, Son to Macduff

ENGLISH FORCES
SIWARD, Earl of Northumberland, General of the English Forces*
SIWARD/YOUNG SIWARD, his son*

MACBETH'S CIRCLE
LADY MACBETH (later, QUEEN)
A PORTER*
SEYTON, servant to Macbeth*
AN ENGLISH DOCTOR*
A SCOTTISH DOCTOR*
GENTLEWOMAN, attending on Lady Macbeth*
AN OLD MAN*

UNDERWORLD
THREE WITCHES
HECATE, Goddess of the Underworld
GHOST OF BANQUO
Apparitions*

SPEAR CARRIERS*
Lords, Gentlemen, Officers, Soldiers, Murderers, Attendants, Messengers

*these parts are often cut, or doubled

CPSIA information can be obtained
at www.ICGtesting.com
Printed in the USA
BVHW080541130822
644512BV00003B/15

9 781408 164624